dining
with
hitler &
hemingway

PLUMB BOB PRESS

FAIRBANKS · ALASKA

Plumb Bob Press
P.O. Box 73561
Fairbanks, Alaska 99707-3561

Cover illustration © 1999 Sam Hamrick
Design by Laura Lucas

Printed in Alaska
ISBN 0-9678572-0-1

dining with hitler & hemingway

stories by
joe karson

for
Lenore Karson

with special thanks to
Laura, Sally & Catherine

stories

papa hemingway's last bullfight

"Fuck Hemingway!"

"Look, he was the best we ever had. Who was better? Come on, who was better?"

"Oh, bullshit! There were dozens of guys better than Hemingway—he just got all the press."

"So why was that? Why did everybody make such a fuss if he was no good? No one knows anything, right? Just you—Mr. Fucking Know-It-All."

"He was an asshole—that's why they made a fuss. He was an asshole, and he made a lot of noise. People like that always get the attention—pick up a newspaper."

"But he could write!"

"He was boring."

"Boring? *Boring*? It was all there—drama, romance, nature."

"Spare me, will you? He was boring. All that crap about hunting and bullfights and—"

"Oh, that's right, you don't approve of bullfighting—too violent. Not like going to one of your precious boxing matches and screaming your fucking head off while two kids beat the shit out of each other—that's okay. And you call other people assholes!"

"A boxing match is a fair fight—either guy can win. How many people you think bet on the bull at a bullfight?"

"The bull wins sometimes."

"How often? If it were a fair fight, half of the time the bull would win. The chickenshit matador takes it every time, so how can you even call it a *fight?* That's illogical—it's a murder."

"Oh! Mr. Logic, now. Selling aluminum siding made you a logic expert.... What you don't understand is that it's the lack of logic that makes the whole thing beautiful."

"What's beautiful about killing some confused animal?"

"The bullfighters get killed too."

"Shit! By the time they're done with the bull, it doesn't have a chance."

"So how come bullfighters get killed? That's all I want to know. If the bull doesn't have a chance, how come matadors get killed?"

"More men get killed by bulls in meatpacking plants than in bullfight rings."

"What?"

"You heard me. They get crushed by the carcasses, pushed into machines. Those are very dangerous places."

"You're full of shit."

"Of course, they're not really bulls, they're mostly steers."

"Bulls, steers, *shmeers*—you're crazy!"

"Look, I'll bet you a hundred dollars that more people are killed each year in meatpacking plants than in bullfight rings."

"Sure, I'll bet you. So how do we find out?"

"Shouldn't be hard. They probably keep records on the bullfights just like we do on baseball."

"What about the other thing?"

"We'll go over to Blue Ribbon Packing—must be someone there who's got some information."

"Okay, but let's make it five hundred."

"Sure, sucker, what do I care?"

■ ■ ■

Frank and Danny had been drinking together and arguing together for over thirty years. Now that they were both retired, that's about all they did. They stepped out of Danny's Ford and looked at the packing plant. It was an ugly old monster with three towering smokestacks. Greasy black smoke spilled from the stacks and settled on the surrounding factories and railroad yards. In front of the plant there was a modern, one-story glass and metal office building.

"That's where we need to go," said Danny, pointing to the newer structure.

"I've got to admit," said Frank, "that place looks awful—but the inside is probably up-to-date and they got all kinds of unions and stuff now."

"I'm telling you, you're better off facing one of those fuckers on the hoof. They carry some poor bastard out of there every day."

"And I'm telling you, you're full of shit."

Frank and Danny entered the office building and walked up to the receptionist's desk. She was using the phone. A plastic nameplate on the desk identified her as Ms. Barlow.

Frank pointed to the nameplate. "What the hell is this 'Ms.' supposed to mean, anyway?"

"It means she's a woman," said Danny.

"That's all it means?"

"Right."

"Jesus!"

Ms. Barlow hung up the phone and smiled at the men. "Can I help you gentlemen with something?"

"We want to know how many people are killed here every year," said Frank.

Ms. Barlow studied Frank for a moment then flashed another big smile. "We kill cattle here, sir, not people."

Frank was about to reply but Danny cut him off.

"We're looking for some statistics on the number of workers who are fatally injured each year in the meatpacking industry."

"Are you men reporters?"

"Yes," said Danny.

"No," said Frank.

Ms. Barlow looked at the men. "I'll tell you what—I think I'm going to let you talk with Mr. Cady, our public relations person. Just walk past that row of desks over there and turn right. His name is on the door."

"Thank you," said Danny.

She punched a button on her intercom as they walked away.

"I don't like that bitch," said Frank.

"They probably just hired her because she's pretty."

"You think she's pretty? Your taste in women is as bad as your taste in writing."

Frank and Danny walked into Mr. Cady's office. He rose slightly from behind a large, neat desk. Cady was about thirty and decked out in expensive new clothing of the most recent style. He adjusted the knot on his tie, then adjusted it again. Mr. Cady tried to smile. Frank examined the man suspiciously.

"Come on in, have some seats."

Frank and Danny moved two chairs closer to the desk and sat down.

"Now, I understand that you have some concerns over plant safety?"

"No," said Danny, "we just want to know how many people get killed here—and at other plants too."

"Killed? To my knowledge there has never been a fatal accident at this plant, if that's what you mean. Now as far as other plants—"

Frank banged his fist down on the desk. "See, what did I tell you!"

"He's lying, you stupid bastard, that's his job!"

"Don't call *me* stupid! The only stupid thing I've done lately is let you drag me to this… 'public relations' office." Frank waved a hand at the room.

"When did I ever *drag* you anywhere? You didn't have to come here with me."

"Sure—I could just let you come here alone and make up some more of your bullshit."

"You saying I'm a liar? You think I'd have to lie to win a bet from *you*?"

"Oh! Abe Lincoln, now. You've never told a lie, right?"

"Hey, if you don't trust me, why don't you just stay the hell out of my life?"

"My pleasure!"

"The trouble with you is, you don't know how to act around people."

"*You*—you're going to tell *me* how to act?"

"You're too ignorant to listen. I'm not telling you anything, anymore."

"Fine. You stay the hell out of *my* life."

"Fine."

"Excuse me," said Mr. Cady, "but could you gentlemen please tell me just who you are?" He reached a hand inside the sleeve of his coat and tugged at his shirt cuff.

"I'll tell you who we are," said Frank. "I'm a man who appreciates great writers—like Hemingway, *Ernest Hemingway*— and this is an illiterate schmuck who thinks he knows everything."

"Have you been drinking?"

Frank stood up. "Of course I've been drinking. You think I sit home watching soap operas and baking bran muffins? Don't you think I'm entitled to some drinks, Mr. Public Relations?"

"Sit down, you old fool," said Danny.

"Don't tell me what to do! I thought you weren't telling me anything, anymore. I thought you were staying out of my life. I thought...." Frank fell back into his chair.

"Frank, I know what day it is today."

"You know shit, that's what you know."

"I know what day it is."

"It's Thursday—you think I'm senile? You think I'm so dumb I don't know what fucking day of the week it is?"

"This is the first time in a year you've gone anywhere but the bar." Danny stared at his friend.

"Forty years. Forty years living with the same woman."

"I know."

"Goddamn it! Stop telling me what you know! Shut up! *Just shut up!*"

"Look, what's this all about?" Mr. Cady had stopped trying to smile.

"It's about Hemingway and his chickenshit bullfighters," said Danny. He spoke slowly, still staring at Frank. "And the suckers that come out of here in plastic bags so we can have pot roast once a week."

"Okay, Mr. Public Relations," said Frank, seated but leaning over the desk. "You've had a good education—what do you think of Hemingway?"

"My name, for your information, is Lawrence Cady, and I—"

"Everyone has a fucking name. Big deal! Tell me what you think of Hemingway."

"I don't know. I'm really not that familiar with the man."

"You never read Hemingway?"

"Wasn't he a poet or something?"

"Jesus Christ!"

"He wrote stories," said Danny. "Didn't they teach you about him in school?"

"I guess so—it's been a while since I read that sort of thing." Mr. Cady adjusted his tie again. He smoothed his lapels.

"Well, you must read *something*," said Frank. "You're supposed to be an educated man, what the hell do you read?"

"I read!"

"Good! So what do you read?"

"I read all the trade journals, I subscribe to several business magazines, and—"

"Oh, I had no idea! A regular Mr. Literature we have here."

"*And*—and I happen to have a very complete home library. My wife has a degree in English and she keeps it stocked with all the best current writing."

"All the best current writing isn't worth a sack of shit. Does your wife buy your ties for you, too?"

"My wife—"

"Hey, Danny, would you look at the tie on this son of a bitch!"

"My wife's taste in writing, *ties*, and everything else is quite excellent, and I don't care to talk about her with a pair of drunks. Now *what* do you men want?"

"Mrs. Taste! A library without any Hemingway and a husband who looks like his mother still dresses him."

"You don't drink, Mr. Cady?" asked Danny.

"I take a drink when I feel like it."

"Don't tell me," said Frank, sipping daintily from an imaginary glass. "You drink Scotch—and always the same fancy brand, right?"

Mr. Cady stood up. "I'd like you men to leave."

"What about all the men who get killed here?" asked Danny.

"I want both of you lunatics out of here *right now!* Or I'll call the police!"

Frank jumped up. "Go ahead! Call the police—call the FBI, call your wife, call your wise-ass secretary, call your mother—"

"Come on," said Danny, "let's get out of here."

Mr. Cady picked up the phone. His hand was shaking.

"No wonder Hemingway shot himself—he couldn't stand to see the world taken over by public relations men!"

Danny grabbed Frank by a sleeve and pulled him out the

door. They walked through the main office again, talking loudly while the secretaries stared. Frank gave Ms. Barlow an evil sneer as they passed her desk. She gave it right back.

"I can't believe he hasn't read Hemingway," said Danny.

"That's the kind of punks they're turning out these days. They have their fancy jobs and their fancy suits—that's all they care about. *Public relations man. Shit!*"

"You'd think they'd come out of school knowing something about the big writers."

Frank and Danny climbed back into the old Ford. If the traffic wasn't too bad, they would make it back to the bar for happy hour.

eating 2

I hold the piece of sushi in front of my face and examine it. Suddenly it hits me. Of course. This is exactly what I am supposed to do. Unlike Oriental cuisines which offer bite-size morsels, Japanese food is presented bite-and-a-half-size. This forces you to study the food while you figure out how to attack it. You have to *experience* the food. This strikes me as being very... *Japanesey.*

I remember the Chinese student my sister once brought home from college with her at Thanksgiving. We couldn't wait to dazzle him with the spectacle of the big roasted bird. When my mother began carving that turkey, Yao turned pale and looked away. He later explained, "In China an animal is butchered before we bring it to the table." Which is true. Americans favor a more hands-on approach. The Japanese seem to follow a middle ground.

"Hey," I announce to my sister and brother-in-law, sitting across the table from me, "I've just had this revelation about the difference between Chinese and Japanese food."

Danny stares at me. I can sense him mentally rolling his eyes. He is not one for cluttering his mind with revelations, especially at mealtime.

"You see, the Chinese disguise their food. They cut everything bite-size so you don't have a chance to really consider what you're shoveling in. The Japanese cut their food a little larger so that you have to hang on to it for more than one bite. This makes you contemplate what you're eating." I look around the restaurant and, sure enough, there is much food hovering between mouths and plates. One diner eyes the remnant of a dumpling that would not quite fit into his mouth. Another peeks awkwardly through a hank of noodles. A man gestures with a shrimp tail. "I think," I continue, "it has something to do with the difference between the cultures."

"Well," says Danny, "that certainly is *food* for thought."

I stare back at him and actually do roll my eyes. My sister remains totally absorbed in her sukiyaki. Sarah is one of those special people. There is barely a hundred pounds to her, but she could eat everything on the table plus a bucket of chicken for dessert, wash it all down with a six-pack, and never burp.

I have been thinking about eating because of my mother. She currently receives all her nourishment through a tube into her stomach. The tube enters her stomach via an incision in her abdomen. She had briefly been attached to the more conventional feeding tube which goes up the nose and down the esophagus but my father grabbed a doctor and told him, "I'll shove a hose up *your* nose and see how *you* like it!" Now she has the direct stomach tube. My mother's illness has been hard on us.

Interestingly, it was eating that first made us aware that my mother was sick again. For the past fifteen years she had been on a strict macrobiotic diet. Really strict. She ate almost nothing but brown rice and steamed vegetables. An occasional slab of roasted tofu and a side of whole-wheat ramen was her idea of shameless splurging—a steak dinner with all the trimmings.

My father came home one night a month ago and found her eating a hamburger. When he asked her about it, she replied testily, "Why shouldn't I eat a hamburger? I always eat hamburgers." My mother's severe regimen was her own alternative to the chemotherapy prescribed for her after a mastectomy. There is little doubt that the diet was effective. One of her doctors, highly skeptical at first, has become a convert to macrobiotics. Eating mush kept her cancer at bay for fifteen years, but now it is back in the form of an inoperable brain tumor. We used to kid my mother about the incredible blandness of her diet. Now her only food is a bag of beige fluid dripped each day into her through a tube.

■ ■ ■

I sit beside my mother's bed, holding her hand. When I squeeze, she squeezes back. I withdraw my hand a ways and let her grope around on the covers until she finds it. We squeeze again. This is how I now communicate with a woman who last month was correcting the grammar of news anchors on network television. She is bundled in a plain white hospital blanket, her eyes mostly fixed straight up at the ceiling. Immobile. Now and then she mutters inaudibly to herself. Occasionally she will startle us both with some random, full-voiced pronouncement. After these outbursts we stare at each other, equally bewildered.

The plump, good-natured attendant comes into the room to clean up my mother. Casually, she is taking the last bite out of a doughnut as she enters. The people who work here amaze me. "Hey, beautiful lady," she drawls, beaming as she approaches the frail wreck of my mother. I move out of the way, and instantly I am struck by a scene from the past.

It was twenty years ago. Out of desperation for employment, I had taken a job as an orderly on the maximum security ward of the Ohio State Mental Hospital. I couldn't imagine a worse job. These men were restricted to the ward and could not use the cafeteria where the other patients ate. Each day at noon their meals would arrive by a dumbwaiter in their own little dining hall. My first lunch on the ward, ground hotdogs with instant mashed potatoes, was served lukewarm on surplus U.S. Army plates that I dealt out to the men as they sat with soupspoons ready in their fists. The long oak table had already been set with stacks of Wonder Bread and pitchers of neon-colored Kool-Aid. They ate heads-down with their chins nearly resting on the table. The stuff went everywhere. Some of the patients had no control of their bodily functions and familiar, foul smells blended into the already overwhelming miasma. Men began shouting and shoving as they fought for the last slices of bread to sop up gravy mixed with spilled Kool-Aid directly from the table top. I knew that I should try to restore order, but I was frozen. By the end of the meal, there was food on the walls, shit smeared across the floor, and vomit, hardly distinguishable from the pre-digested food, dripping from the table and chairs. My God! I was trying to force my shaking legs to carry me out of the hall for some air when the nurse who cared for these men came over to me and said, "Now, honey, don't you be wasting your money on meals down in the commissary. They always send up a couple extra plates in the dumbwaiter. You just go over there and grab yourself one." I nodded my thanks and lurched away. I was certain that I would never be able to eat again in my life. Looking at my mother's feeding tube, I'm feeling that way again.

My father and sister enter the room while the attendant tucks my mother back into her covers. As soon as she leaves, my father is standing over the bed, talking to my mother like they were back home in their kitchen. She blurts something out and he throws his hands up toward my sister.

"Why does she say these things? She says her mother is in the other room. Her mother's been dead for thirty years."

I grip my chair and stare down at the floor. I want to grab

my father and shout, "DO YOU THINK MAYBE IT'S BECAUSE SHE HAS A BRAIN TUMOR? DO YOU THINK MAYBE THAT'S WHY SHE SAYS THESE THINGS?" But I don't. I just sit staring at the floor. My father is reacting to this crisis in his usual manner—by refusing to accept it. This has always been his way. He had watched my mother eat hamburgers for a full week before mentioning it to anyone. There must have been other equally disturbing changes in her behavior. I know that his denial springs from a genuine devotion to my mother and this is what allows me to control my anger. I do not want to lock horns with him again, as we have in the past over so many things. This is no time to start an argument and I won't. But I still grip the chair.

My sister is reading the situation. She convinces my father that he needs to eat something, and she will accompany him to the hospital cafeteria. When he asks me to join them, I say that I have already eaten. This is a lie. I'm beginning to think about the bar I have discovered around the corner that pours an honest shot of Irish whiskey. I look up at the bag of crud dripping into my mother. I too am currently favoring a liquid diet. Whiskey is nothing but distilled water and grain. According to my mother's books, it's macrobiotic.

■ ■ ■

I am at my parents' house, alone with my father. I'm trying to teach him how to feed himself. It's not easy.

He tells me there is nothing to eat.

I tell him, "There's ham in the refrigerator and a fresh loaf of bread on the counter. Does that suggest something?"

"But it's white bread," he says. "Doesn't ham go on rye?"

"When you're hungry, ham will go quite nicely on whatever bread is around." I am prepared to continue the lesson but stop. I realize that I can take nothing for granted. In his seventy-six years, this man has never made a sandwich. First my grandmother made them for him and for the next fifty years it was my mother's job. Things were simple for his generation: men worked and women made sandwiches. Even during her macrobiotic years, my mother fixed all his meals. And he would not meet her halfway by eating rice with his pork chops. It had to be potatoes as usual. She did not seem to mind. When they traveled, she often ate rice in their RV and then sat with him in restaurants while he had his steak. There was no problem. It still amazes me that they were able to function this way. They just plain did not allow a difference in eating habits to interfere with their companionship. They made things work. This was another side of my father's simpler generation.

I decide to drop the sandwich lesson.

My father says he is tired of everyone telling him that he is not eating right. The garbage can is full of untouched salads and vegetable casseroles that keep showing up at the house. I tell him to eat what he wants. There is nothing wrong with the TV dinners and frozen pastries I have taught him to prepare in the microwave. Food is food and you have to eat. "What are they worried about?" I ask him. "That you'll die young?"

We both laugh.

"I'd rather choke on a T-bone today," he says, "than live another twenty years on hay."

I tell him that I agree. It feels good to be laughing with my father, to be on the same side for once. Then I remember the avocado.

"What happened to that avocado?" I ask. My sister had brought him an avocado, thinking it might be the one vegetable he would eat, and left it on the kitchen counter. It was gone.

"The what?"

"The avocado— that dark green thing that was on the counter."

"Oh, that. I thought it was something you found in the yard—I threw it out."

Lord! I had assumed that even my father would recognize

an avocado. But why? His favorite place to eat is still Lenny's Grill, located in a bowling alley. Lenny's specialties are chicken-fried steak and a grilled baloney sandwich considered by many to be the finest in central Ohio. The *Number One* on the breakfast menu is Coffee and Cigarettes. Lenny probably doesn't do much with avocados.

■ ■ ■

We all leave the hospital together: my sister, my brother-in-law, my father and myself. My sister has made reservations for dinner at the Japanese restaurant again, and tonight our father will be coming along. We don't think he should be alone. My mother has had a bad day, not responding to anything. None of us is in a good mood. My father is impossible.

On the way to dinner, in the back of Danny's car, I tell my father how the Jade Garden was my mother's favorite restaurant. I used to take her there for lunch because it is one of the only places in town that serves food she could eat on her diet. My father doesn't care. He is not going to eat anything with eyeballs still in it. Didn't the Japanese try to kill him for two years when he was a soldier in the Philippines? He is not eating on the floor, he hates tea, rice sticks to his dental work, and why would anyone eat raw fish?

I tell him that we are not sitting on the floor. There will be tables just like anywhere else. And they have beef. He can probably even get it overcooked, just the way he likes it. It's no use. He continues to fume.

Things do not improve for my father at the restaurant. He dismisses the miso soup as "sludge." No, he would not like an appetizer—he is not eating anything with tentacles.

"Mushrooms do not have tentacles," I tell him. "Even in Japan."

He waves the back of his hand at me.

When our entrées arrive, my father is a little happier. Beef teriyaki is something he can almost understand. I have already instructed the waitress to bring him a fork.

My father holds up a bite-and-a-half-size piece of beef. Hungry for the first time in days, I have packed away three of my shrimp tempura when I notice that he has not moved. He is still staring at the fork, just inches from his mouth, but something has changed. The hardness I have grudgingly grown to respect, perhaps even love, is gone from my father's face. His eyes are no longer narrowed by anger but by pain. Suddenly, all the frustrations of his new world seem to be concentrated at the end of a fork. Aware that I am looking at him, my father shifts his mouth from one side of the fork to the other, as if still searching for a way to attack the slightly too large morsel of meat. He stops and just stares again but his eyes are now focused on nothing I can see. His head slowly drops down toward the table. I watch as his shoulders begin to tremble then quake.

blind lemon assenmacher: amish bluesman

Got me a black cat quilt
Got me a mojo whip
Gonna hitch up my buggy
Take a long long trip
I got the blues….

Blind Lemon Assenmacher is on his front porch singing and playing guitar. The porch is white like every other porch in Holmes County. Blind Lemon is dressed in black. There's no rule about guitars, and Blind Lemon's is candy-apple red. It's a good copy of a 1957 Les Paul, refitted with twin split-coil Mighty Mite humbuckers, Tune-O-Matic bridge, and Parsons-White string bender. His 100 watt MESA/Boogie amp is set at only 5, but in Blind Lemon's mind, the system is always cranked right up to 10. In his mind, it is also plugged in. Due to a lack of electricity, the equipment has never truly been tested, but it's a serious rig, and Blind Lemon knows exactly what it should sound like. Playing unplugged has made his ear incredibly sharp. When he turns eighteen next year, and splits the farm, he might still practice this way just to keep his edge. Blind Lemon executes a lightning arpeggio through an E major seventh chord and mentally blasts it against the dark, solemn hills surrounding the Assenmacher homestead. His famous "Jericho Lick." He taps the Mister Crybaby Deluxe wah-wah pedal by his right boot. It's his gift to be simple, so this is the only electronic effect he employs. Blind Lemon favors a lean, soaring, Delta-wail type of sound. He knows when that sound is working because he'll get a certain feeling down in his feet. Those feet have never been outside Holmes County, Ohio, but he knows that what he's feeling is pure Mississippi mud oozing up between his toes. When he was only five, he startled his family one fall evening by suddenly jumping barefoot into a vat of apple butter, wiggling his toes around, and letting out a long, mournful howl. Livestock out in the pasture instinctively huddled together. His six siblings stared in corn-fed, apple-cheeked awe. Papa Assenmacher's bible dropped to the floor. His mama beamed: "B-flat—and such righteous tone!"

Little girl with the black dress on
She can churn my butter all night long
Used to churn my butter 'til my knees got weak
Now she see me comin'
She just turn the other cheek
I got the blues....

Blind Lemon Assenmacher's vocal style is not entirely free from local influences. His singing includes strong elements of Snuffling Hog, Snoring Deacon, Burbling Syrup, and Simon Yoder's Tractor. The Yoders are a notorious tribe of jack-Amish whose farm borders the Assenmachers'. They have a tractor outfitted with wagon wheels, thus circumventing the rule on field equipment which merely bans pneumatic tires. Since no one knows how to maintain the thing, it sputters and bucks along with only half its cylinders firing and is often aided in its erratic locomotion by a team of terrified horses. It is loathed by the rest of the community. Blind Lemon has found the abused mechanical beast to be a unique source of inspiration.

I'm your little red tractor, mama
Mama let me plant-UNH! plant-UNH!
Mama let me plant-UNH! my seed
If you'd only grease my axle, mama
UNH! You know I'd give you what you need.

I'm you're love machine, mama
But you got-UNH! got-UNH!
You gotta keep-UNH! my chassis oiled
You done stripped all my gears
UNH! And now you let my water boil.

I'm your little red tractor, mama
Mama let me....

Blind Lemon is lost in his onomatopoetic tribute to Simon Yoder's tractor when his parents step out onto the porch. Papa Assenmacher is a slight man, dressed in overalls and a black coat that fit as if they were passed down from a bigger brother. His gaunt, weathered features are nearly hidden under a wide straw hat. He looks like something whittled from a sweat-stained hoe handle. His wife looks like something you could eat: bread-loaf body, dumpling arms, marzipan face, powdered sugar hair. Mama Assenmacher nods her head and snaps her fingers to the music. Papa glares at his son over his spectacles.

"Mama, why must he embarrass us like this?"

"He's just working on his chops, Papa. A boy's got to keep up his chops, don't he?"

Papa Assenmacher continues to glare. "And what about this blind business? The boy sees better than any of us."

"Oh, Papa. It's just a trip—it'll pass. Lots of teenage boys think they're blind."

"All that time he spends alone in his room, he probably *is* going blind."

Blind Lemon launches into a blistering atonal riff, aiming the guitar at his speaker stack and wincing at the feedback that should be there.

Papa Assenmacher winces, too. "Well, why can't he at least play something nice—like a polka."

Blind Lemon suddenly stops playing. Mama Assenmacher bites her lip and kneads her hands into her apron. Legend has it that Blind Lemon once heard a polka on the Yoders' wind-up Victrola. When told that this was the music of his ancestors, he became so distraught that he shunned his mother's rich Germanic cooking for an entire year. This "Beans and Greens Period" may be responsible for metabolic disturbances that affected Blind Lemon's still developing vocal chords. It is thought to have been a factor in producing his distinctive singing voice.

Blind Lemon plucks a corn-silk cigarette from the peghead of his guitar. He strikes a wooden match on his boot and lights up, slowly turning to face his father. Jaws clenched, his goat-bearded chin thrust upward, Papa Assenmacher strides toward his son. He stops with his hat brim pressed right against Blind Lemon's silver wraparound shades. The man plumps himself up, straining to fill the bib of his overalls. Blind Lemon drags on his cigarette as father and son silently confront each other. The only sound is the sizzling and popping corn silk. Blind Lemon exhales out the corner of his mouth.

"Let's go eat!" says Mama, grabbing for her son's sleeve. "Come on—food's on the table. We'll all feel better after we've had a nice dinner."

Blind Lemon pulls away. Cigarette dangling, he sits down on a milk can and begins playing to the hills. Effortlessly, his voice modulates into the rich, Snoring Deacon mode.

Don't want no schnitzels
Don't want no noodles
Don't want no brats
Don't want no strudels
I got the blues....

sunday

"Listen to those birds sing."

"They're not singing—they're screaming."

"Screaming?"

"Sure."

"Why do you have to ruin everything?"

"I'm just being realistic. If you were put in a little cage like that, what would you do—sing or scream?"

"Forget it."

Paul and Janet walked toward the gerbil cages. One of the rodents was working out in its exercise wheel, and though Janet always found that amusing, she knew better than to say anything. Paul would explain again that the gerbil wasn't playing, that it ran in the wheel because it was crazy from being confined.

"I don't think animals like that are smart enough to go crazy," said Janet.

"What?"

Paul stared at Janet. He squinted, tilting his head in mock

confusion. Janet hated that look. He knew perfectly well what she was talking about.

"Their brains are too simple."

"*What?*"

More of that look—innocence mixed now with just a hint of irritation. He was going to push it, punish her for being a sloppy communicator.

"Never mind."

The rabbits were next. Janet had once called the baby rabbits "cute" and set Paul off on a discourse about the relativity of cuteness: "Why is a baby rabbit or seal cuter than a baby snake? If we trapped or clubbed baby snakes no one would care, but...."

It was Janet who had originally requested that they include the pet store in their Sunday browsing routine. She loved animals. Now, visiting them was just another chore. She actually felt relieved that this was always their shortest stop.

Janet followed Paul through the tropical fish section while he gave each tank a quick looking-over. Paul was interested in fish, but after they were dead and laid out on ice.

■ ■ ■

Janet braced herself as they entered Lee's Fish Market. It was owned by Koreans or Vietnamese, she could never remember. The store contained all the varieties of fish and seafood imaginable and some that could have been from another world. There were live lobsters, crabs, and other crawling things, and a tank filled with tiny fish like minnows. Paul had told her once that you were supposed to swallow them alive. Most of the fish, however, were quite dead and the sudden blast of ammonia-laced fish rot stung Janet's eyes and caught in her throat. This was, according to Paul, "a serious fish market."

Lee's was part of what had become an unchanging Sunday ritual. First, there was coffee and rolls and the *Times* at the

Green Parrot. Paul and Janet always arrived at eleven, the busiest time of the day, and waited in line outside the café for half an hour. Janet could never help staring through the big picture window at the people already seated inside. They seemed to have a special attitude, a serenity that was the reward for being where others wanted to be. It was easy to imagine that they sipped their coffee and read their newspapers at a deliberately slow pace. Like the other couples in the line, Paul and Janet spoke very little while they waited. It was as if everyone felt embarrassed at being caught on the outside looking in and did not want to be conspicuous. Once inside, where they really belonged, they would all relax and be more sociable. Janet wished that it were so. She found the atmosphere in the Green Parrot, with its cold, impersonal service, the customers so crowded yet so distant and formal, scarcely an improvement over the sidewalk. The first few times they came here she had thought the whole thing to be humorous—people standing in line to get a cup of coffee and read the biggest paper they could find in the most cramped, uncomfortable space they could find. Now she simply dreaded the place. She remembered the Sundays of her childhood with the funnies spread out on the living-room floor while breakfast cooked in the kitchen. The rug, the colored ink, the frying bacon all blending into the smell of Sunday morning. Janet wondered if anyone else in the Green Parrot had such memories.

After the Green Parrot, Paul and Janet toured the same series of shops and galleries with the pet store always next to last and Lee's the final stop. Here in the fish market, at least, there was a range of interesting people for Janet to watch while Paul made his selection of the evening's fare, a process that could take an hour. The people in the café and in the neat little shops all looked the same, acted the same. At Lee's the customers rivaled the exotic displays that brought them thronging in from both ends of the long, tunnel-like building. Many of the customers were Oriental, and it seemed to Janet that they were always angry. She watched an old woman pick up a fish from a trough of ice then instantly slam it back down, shaking her head. Another old woman, standing behind the trough in a blood-stained apron, spat something out at her and threw up her hands. The customer mimicked the gesture before storming away as best she could in painful, mincing little steps. All over the market, similar transactions took place.

Janet hurried past a pile of plump, thick-lipped carp, fish that looked like they belonged in a cartoon, as she headed for the one part of the market that offered some relief from the smell. An advantage of having spent so much time in here was that she actually knew her way around the incredible maze of offal. She could almost smell her way around. At the stall filled with packaged and canned delicacies, Janet stopped and pretended to search for an item. My God, she thought, the things people eat! A short, round man without any teeth stood next to her staring up at a shelf. Janet looked. There was a large bottle up there, like the bottle for a water cooler, filled with grinning eel-like creatures embalmed in a sick yellow fluid. Janet winced involuntarily. Her chin snapped down into her tightly hunched shoulder. She was shaking, and she knew that the little round man was watching her, but she didn't care. She wanted to be away from there, away from people who ate things like that. Where was Paul? She hadn't seen him in twenty minutes and had no idea where he was. It was cold in there, it smelled, and she was alone.

■ ■ ■

Janet dropped into a chair at the kitchen table and sat motionless while Paul pulled packages out of a shopping bag and lined them up on the counter. On some Sundays, he would have only one heavy package to show for all the time spent at the market. Sometimes, like today, there would be several tiny packages which meant that he was going to cook a bouillabaisse or a fancy stew. Paul's seafood dinners completed the Sunday ritual: serious café, serious fish market, and now—the serious cooking. Janet could tell by the number of packages that dinner was going to be a long, complicated affair. She would end up having to wash every pot in the kitchen. Once a week, Paul was a chef, and a chef could not be expected to clean up after himself. She had been hoping for just a slab of baked fish.

Paul was suddenly all over the kitchen—jerking drawers open, flinging pantry doors. The energy that Janet felt draining from her body seemed to flow directly into Paul. Janet fought briefly to keep her attention in the room, then let herself drift away. She imagined herself at one of her family's fish fries with batter-dipped perch fresh from the crackling oil and shameless mounds of tartar sauce—the kind made from bottled mayonnaise and relish that Paul condemned as an "insult to any decently prepared fish." When was the last time she had tasted *real* tartar sauce?

"Hey!" Paul poked Janet's shoulder with his finger. "What's the matter? You're not crapping out on me, are you?"

Janet straightened up in the chair and tried to focus on Paul as he dropped a skillet onto a burner with more noise than was necessary. Having an audience was part of the Sunday fish finale, and there was no napping during performances. Since they began walking home, Janet had stuck to Paul like a lost pup, but she felt as alone as she had back at the market. She watched Paul moving along the counter, opening each package with a magician's flourish. He seemed so strange. It might as well have been the little round man without any teeth there in the kitchen with her.

Paul made a quarter-turn at the counter, like a teacher about to lecture his class from a blackboard.

"The whiting looked so good that I thought at first we might have a simple Merlan a l'anglaise, but then I found these wonderful mussels. When I spotted the butter clams, I knew that a Bouillabaisse Normande…."

Janet nodded her head without hearing a word.

5
dog story

Boomer walked through the snow thinking about Suzy. He had been thinking about Suzy all day: those blue eyes with the long, soft lashes and, of course, the tail. Mostly it was the tail—fat and fluffy, just the way Boomer liked them. Suzy had come into heat two days ago and broken the chain that kept her in the dog yard with the other sled dogs. Now she was alone and free up in the hills above the frozen river. She was a wily old bitch and her owner had failed in all his attempts to lure her back. Boomer would have no trouble finding her—just follow the furrow left in the snow by the trailing length of chain and inhale that delicious scent.

Boomer headed up the hill with his nose down in the furrow. So intent was Boomer in following the trail up to Suzy that he didn't notice the two wolves approaching across the side of the hill. Suddenly there was a new but familiar scent—Boomer looked up at the wolves standing in front of him. One was a large animal and the other young or stunted. They were mangy, sneaky-looking brutes with grinning fangs and tails that arched down between their legs.

Shit! thought Boomer, just my luck. Boomer was a good-sized, healthy Labrador, and he knew that he had a chance against one wolf in the middle of winter when they were weak from lack of food. These guys looked pretty bad off, but with two, even that small one, there wasn't much hope.

"Hey, wimp, where you think you're going?" said the bigger wolf.

"Wimp," said the smaller one.

"If you're thinking of visiting that sweet little husky up there you can just forget it—we'll be handling that."

"Yeh, *we'll* handle it," repeated the small wolf. He was drooling terribly.

What a disgusting runt, thought Boomer. If his big friend gives him a turn at all, that fool will probably lock up inside Suzy, and they'll both freeze to death before I can get a little myself.

"Besides," continued the big wolf, "she's not your type. She's a working girl—from the other side of the tracks, just like us guys." The wolves looked at each other and snickered.

Boomer hated that old line of crap. He flushed grouse for his master in the fall, he barked when strangers came around. That was work. Boomer growled.

"Ooh, tough guy! Listen, you better just trot your little housebroken ass home and be thankful we're in a hurry. If you're still around when we finish with the bitch, we're going to kick your butt good. Dipshit!"

"Dipshit!" said the runt.

Boomer growled again and took a step toward the little wolf who jumped back. That felt good. But the bigger wolf started coming at him, and there was nothing to do but retreat down the hill. It was humiliating. Boomer gave a last half-hearted growl over his shoulder and headed home.

Working his way down the hill, Boomer listened to the taunts of the wolves as they swaggered off: "Maybe if you sit up and beg like a good little doggie, your master will give you a biscuit." "Curl up by your smelly stove and lick yourself!" "Yeh, lick yourself!" "Go fetch a stick, sucker!"

It was hard to take, but soon Boomer would be back at the cabin, and his rug by the stove *was* starting to sound pretty good. The boss had shot a moose a few days ago, and if he didn't fuck up for a while, maybe there'd be a bone in it for him.

6

jackpot

I really hit the jackpot. His name was Bill Tiffin and he was a dairy technology major. He actually had pictures of cows taped to the walls. Okay, in 1963 most pinups had a certain cow-like quality, but I mean, these were Holsteins, Guernseys, whatever. I was a first-semester freshman at Ohio State University, and Bill was my roommate. He had already settled into our gleaming cubicle in Stanley Hall, newest of O.S.U.'s modern high-rise dormitories, when I arrived. My reception was a bit unnerving. Why all the raised eyebrows and other sly, smug gestures from the suspiciously large and jovial crew of well-wishing students that had gathered to greet me in front of room 712? Why were strangers giving me a hero's welcome at my new home? Like I said, I really hit the jackpot.

Let me try to describe Bill Tiffin. The first thing you would notice, well, maybe after the hair, was Bill's skin. It is necessary here to invoke an image of the unborn or the deceased because there is nothing in the range between these that will serve as a model for the man's complexion. It was a complexion that I had previously associated with things floating in jars in my high-school biology lab. It was a horror-film complexion. The first time I saw Bill Tiffin's face, I imagined a chill mist rising from an old graveyard, the sudden burst of bat wings and shrieking pipe-organ chords. A ghostly blue-white paste coated that featureless face—a face as cold and blank as a hunk of rancid dough. I felt like I could knead it with my fingers into any expression I wished and it would just stay that way. Not that the clammy clay of Bill Tiffin's neutral countenance would invite any such intimacy. Though smooth and unblemished, this was not skin you would deliberately touch. Two limp, shapeless limbs fashioned from the same unwholesome batter hung through the drooping pits of Bill Tiffin's dull white T-shirt. It clung in random folds and bulges to his slight frame, creating a shoulderless, waistless, hipless form that was at once both frail and flabby. How had any living person acquired so deathly a texture? How had the lush, sparkling green hills of Ohio dairyland produced an eighteen-year-old resembling an embalmed grub?

Now for the hair. Bill Tiffin's hair was not really blond but, like his skin, merely lacking in pigment. He wore it so close-cropped that at first sight he seemed bald— almost. There was, of course, that business in the front. There was that single feature, that one ornament contrived by the formless, colorless Bill Tiffin to hail his otherwise perfectly bland presence. He grew the hair just above his forehead to an amazing six-inch length, waxed it, and combed it straight forward in the manner of a bill. Indeed, with his shaved head, the hatless Bill Tiffin appeared to be wearing a cap. If you were of average height, this stiff, dirty yellow hair-bill pointed toward your chin when you confronted the man. It completed the near total obscurity of his tiny, subterranean eyes. Eyes that, from what little I could see of them, had the color and vitality of a dirty aquarium. Now throw in some baggy, faded, hand-me-down clothing, and you will have a fair picture of my eccentric and—I am not afraid to say—faintly extraterrestrial roommate, Bill Tiffin.

I accepted my fate philosophically. Okay, with ten thousand new students arriving at O.S.U. that fall, I had drawn the prize geek for a roommate. But it was like not having a roommate at all. There was no more substance to Bill Tiffin's silent personality than there was to his pathetic body. He was invisible, not really there—even though he was *always* there. You see, Bill almost never left the room. Now, with any other person, this would have been a problem. A serious problem. Not with Bill Tiffin. I rapidly grew to regard him as little more than another piece of furniture, something that came with the room. He was scarcely more animate or conversant. Mostly, he just sat on his bed polishing the shiny black shoes and brass badges that belonged to his R.O.T.C. uniform. Bill Tiffin lived for R.O.T.C. and that uniform.

Let me tell you about R.O.T.C. The Reserve Officers' Training Corps, known to most as ROT-SEE, was a big thing at Ohio State. All male freshmen and sophomores were required to enroll in R.O.T.C. It had something to do with the government giving money to the school. If you stayed in the program for your final two years, Uncle Sam paid all your expenses, and you went into the army as a second lieutenant when you graduated. The initial R.O.T.C. obligation involved one class each week in military science, whatever the hell that is, and wearing a uniform instead of your regular clothes every Monday. What a way to start the week. The uniforms were these thick wool surplus jobs from World War II that smelled like mothballs when they were dry and piss when they were wet. A lot of guys went to Ohio State because of R.O.T.C. I wanted no part of it.

The whole military thing was just not my cup of tea, but to be truthful, it was the uniform that I absolutely could not handle. The fact that everyone wore them did little to comfort me. I had my own serious ideas about how a man should present himself in public—all seven days of the week. Which is to say, if I may be even more truthful, that what this was really about was girls. Girls were important to me as a freshman at O.S.U. I had never seen so many of them. They were everywhere, thousands of them. They overran the whole town, filled the campus, were right there in class with you where you could look at them, smell them, touch them, and even talk to them—if you were not in some ill-fitting, piss-stinking uniform.

So, I had a problem. Since I was a freshman, R.O.T.C. was mandatory, like living in the dorm. But it was right there on the seventh floor of Stanley Hall that I found my savior. His name was Rick the Prick, and his room was just two doors down from my own. Rick the Prick was the highest ranking student in the advanced R.O.T.C. program. He was the boss. A natural gift for giving orders and being unpleasant had easily carried him to that exalted position and earned him his name. I was not impressed. Despite his official status and fearsome title, I figured that any senior who still lived in the dorm had to be a loser at heart. If I could just find a weakness, I knew that I would be able to manipulate Rick the Prick for my own purposes. This turned out to be rather simple.

You see, Rick the Prick also had a problem. It was the English language—as it applied off of a drill field, in general, and in college-level composition courses, in particular. To graduate and thus receive his commission in the U.S. Army, Rick the Prick still had to complete the English 101 composition course he had been putting off for four years. The prospect of committing words to paper terrified this man more than anything in the world. A lot of guys suffered with this problem, but Rick the Prick really had it bad. This is where I came in.

Fortunately, like Rick the Prick, I too possessed a gift. I could write. Unfortunately, it was my fate to be born into a generation that really had mathematics shoved down its throat. At a time when everyone wanted to be a nuclear physicist or rocket scientist, I had squeaked through high school barely able to add or subtract without using my fingers. Algebra? Calculus? Forget it. I was as bad with numbers as Rick the Prick was with words. But I could write. It just came to me without any effort at all. As a matter of fact, I scored so high on the written part of my college entrance exams that I was given full credit for all my required freshman English courses. In my entire college career, I would never have to write a single English composition—unless I wanted to. Or there was something in it for me.

Rick the Prick and I had no trouble striking a deal. I made sure that the first composition I wrote for him was a dandy. It scored an *A* and that was when I really owned the man—body, mind, and olive drab soul. If any of his following papers showed a decline in quality, he would be exposed as a cheat. He would be thrown out of school and lose his officer's commission. His glorious future as a leader of men and a prick would be ended right there. Undoubtedly, he would return to Goober Junction, Ohio, where he would marry his homely high school sweetheart, raise three subnormal children, and go for the gold watch at the local manure works. He would probably have difficulty being a prick in his own home. Rick the Prick saw to it that all the proper paperwork went through that showed me as having completed my R.O.T.C. obligation. I would not have to play soldier. I would not have to wear that horrible uniform or shell out for the big fat book on military science, whatever the hell that is. So much for me and R.O.T.C.

Well, like I said, Bill Tiffin rarely left the room. We still had those damn cows on the wall, but once Bill got his uniform, he lost all enthusiasm for the dairy business, and, so it seemed, everything else in the world. He just sat there polishing those ugly shoes and phony badges. Except for R.O.T.C., he never went to a class. His only other routine excursions off the bed were a trip once a day to our cafeteria for the evening meal, and a disappearing act he pulled for a few hours each Sunday afternoon. I will get to that Sunday thing in a bit. First, let me tell you about Bill Tiffin's dinner ritual.

Bill would line up every evening with the rest of the guys to load his tray. Stanley Hall dinners featured your standard dry-cleaned meat, murdered vegetables, creative Jell-O work, et cetera, and he scooped up hearty portions of everything, including dessert. He always took a double helping of mashed potatoes, topped with a spoonful of pale, flour-laced gravy. This was ordinary enough behavior, and though Bill Tiffin had no friends, he seldom dined alone. As soon as he headed for a table with his tray, several big jock-types would fall in behind him like a pack of jackals sensing a kill. They were never disappointed. Once seated, he instantly cast off all of his food except for the mashed potatoes, a few slices of white bread, and a glass of milk. He consumed the potatoes and dry, unbuttered bread, then took one tiny sip of the milk, rolling it around in his mouth like a wine connoisseur assessing a new vintage. This was Bill Tiffin's daily intake of food. I do not see how the man stayed alive. Even in its nourishment, his body was simply the enemy of all color and substance.

Now, about the Sunday afternoons. These were special for Bill Tiffin. Every Sunday, around noon, he would suit up in the finest of his tired old clothes, which were the best argument I had seen for the R.O.T.C. uniform, perform a particularly conscientious wax job on his bill, and splash on two or three varieties of after-shave lotion. I almost forgot to tell you about the after-shave lotion. Along with R.O.T.C. and a devotion to looking like the champion geek in the history of Ohio State University, after-shave lotion was the one other big thing in Bill Tiffin's life. We each had two built-in drawers in our dorm room and he filled both of his with bottles of the stuff. I never knew that there were so many different kinds. He had them all—Canoe, Old Spice, Lilac Vegetal, English Leather, Timberline, Stetson, five brands of bay rum. It was only on Sunday that I ever actually saw him apply any of the fragrances. After he was properly dressed, waxed, and perfumed, he would disappear.

Where did Bill Tiffin go? Given the usual implications of after-shave lotion, it would seem logical to surmise that he was rendezvousing with a member of the opposite sex. This was out of the question—although conjuring up a female counterpart to Bill Tiffin was certainly entertaining. He had never been within ten of his waxed-hair-bill-lengths of a female in his life. For that matter, the cadaver-skinned farmboy had never shaved in his life. So where did Bill Tiffin go? I could hardly help pondering this matter and fortunately, for the sake of my curiosity, I was not alone. Because of his celebrity geekhood, there were several Bill Tiffin watchers. One of the more ambitious of these spies, obviously a serious geek himself, provided me with the solution to this little mystery. What Bill Tiffin did on Sunday afternoons was—nothing. He would take a bus into downtown Columbus and first lounge for a while in a park by the statehouse. Next, he did some window-shopping, mostly checking out the variety stores and pharmacies for new developments in shoe polish and after-shave lotion. Since the dorm did not feed us on Sunday, he topped off the big day with dinner at a fairly decent restaurant. Always the same one. Perhaps he had found a chef who mashed a particularly mean potato.

I have already mentioned that I thought I did quite well at accepting my jackpot roommate. Still, I was not beyond trying to, well, steer him a little when it came to certain issues. For instance, I pointed out to Bill that all of his polishing and buffing was a waste of time. Since he never went to any classes, he was going to flunk out of school. Instead of becoming an officer, he would end up a grunt foot soldier, and given the times, probably in short order. Here, I was bluffing a bit. I figured that no army in the world would accept a specimen like Bill Tiffin, but who knew? There was more or less a war going on, and he was more or less a warm body. Also, I suggested to him that he might pay a little more attention to his nutrition. Perhaps if he beefed up some, things would start going better for him. During these roommate-to-roommate sessions, I would crouch down to get my eyes beneath that damn hair visor of his, but it was hard to tell if you were ever really getting through.

He just sat there on the edge of his bed, contentedly, I am tempted to say *bovinely*, rubbing away with his polishing rag. Maybe he had simply been too long with cows. Maybe *I* was the one wasting my time—but you see, I really did not want Bill Tiffin to flunk out of school. I did not want to lose him for a roommate. Especially when I considered the alternatives. The women at Ohio State University in the fall of 1963 were all genuine goddesses, but the men, as far as I could see, were not much. If Bill Tiffin went, he would undoubtedly be replaced by some preppy fraternity punk, goon-mutant jock, or unnecessarily cheerful Bible-thumper. This was mostly what you had for men around there. Bill Tiffin could be exasperating, but I did not relish sharing a room with any of these other types.

Of course, some were less tolerant of Bill Tiffin than myself. About halfway through the fall semester, my roommate stopped bothering to dress on a regular basis. Clad now in only his shorts or a towel, he persisted in his heroic inactivity, and it was then that the maids began refusing to clean the room. I cannot say that I blamed them. It was also about then that I had my first run-in with Andrew Ferguson, Stanley Hall's resident student counselor. Disturbing reports concerning my roommate had finally reached Andrew, and he asked me to meet with him in his office.

I disliked the man. For one thing, he insisted on being called Andrew, instead of Andy, and what does that tell you about someone? Also, how many thirty-five-year-old men would want to spend all of their time in a college dormitory? He was one of those guys who was just too perfect. Perfectly tailored Ivy-League clothes, perfectly trimmed hair, perfect teeth. Even the pennies in his loafers gleamed. You just knew that he always sent his mother a card on Mother's Day, flossed regularly, never drank, and said his prayers at night. There he was, sitting at his perfect desk. Directly behind him was this painting of a fifty-story-tall Jesus knocking on the side of the U.N. Building. Nice. Andrew gave me a big phony smile. "So," he asked, "how is Bill Tiffin doing?" "Just fine," I said. "He's insane, dying of malnutrition, setting a new record for flunking courses that would barely challenge a well-trained Labrador retriever, and eagerly anticipating the chance to have his creamy white ass shot off in some fetid Vietnamese rice paddy." Andrew just looked at me. He was not a man who appreciated picturesque speech—unless it came from the King James version of the Bible. Among his other bad habits, Andrew Ferguson was an evangelist. He was yet another of the religious fanatics that seemed to infest that whole school. Andrew told me that maybe I could assist my roommate through the difficult time he was experiencing. This idea got him started on some tedious Biblical parable which, in turn, led to an endless account of his glorious Scottish ancestry. What had I done to deserve all this? It was torture. You see, I have always been bored by people who make a big thing out of the happenstance of their birth. If you want to impress me, you will have to tell me what you have done, not who you are. But Andrew went on and on until I thought he was going to jump up on his desk and dance a fling. Then he suddenly stopped and gave me that look again. "Of course," he said, "given your well-known weaknesses for drinking beer and chasing women, you are something less than the ideal person to be assisting anyone." I gave Andrew one of my own looks. I informed him that my beer-drinking and woman-chasing merely filled in the time that I would have spent on the English classes from which I had been excused. That got him. I did not normally like to flaunt my achievements but, if pressed, I was not above bringing them into play. Furthermore, I assured him that I had already taken it upon myself to help my roommate and felt, sadly, that it was a hopeless cause— possibly even for someone with higher moral standards than my own. Andrew said he would pray for Bill Tiffin. "Amen," I added.

I was not ashamed of what Andrew referred to as my "weaknesses." Especially one of them. I told you that girls were important to me, and why not? A particular girl, Susan, was very important. I had approached the wondrously silken-haired, full-chested Susan after a class we shared, and she agreed to have coffee with me. On our way to the coffee shop, we somehow ended up in the bushes down at Echo Lake, just doing what came naturally. At least what came naturally to me. I could not speak for the other male students at O.S.U. who, like I said, did not strike me as much. They seemed rather slow in matters such as detours into the bushes, but that was just fine with me.

The main problem I had with women was figuring out where to take them. Sex in the bushes was certainly better than none at all, but I was tired of making love like some damn animal. When you think of it, making love in a bed is one of the things that *separates* people from animals. And I had never had that pleasure. My only experiences so far were on the ground, the beach, in cars, on a picnic table, even a putting green. I got caught on that last one and had to pay the golf course for tearing up the grass so badly, but that is quite a story in itself.

Anyway, I was determined to pleasure myself with Susan in a real bed. I slept each night, of course, in a perfectly fine bed—a bed that for the first time in my life I was paying to use. I had worked hard to make the money for my college tuition which included the room in Stanley Hall and that bed. Now, if I paid for it, it was *my* bed, and it struck me that I should be able to use it for anything I wished. So what was I still doing in the bushes? The more I dwelled on this matter, the more determined I became to raise my sex life off the ground and put it into a bed, *my* bed, where it belonged. I deserved this. I had a highly developed sense of justice and I knew my rights. It was this sort of thinking that led to the big fuss which is really what this whole thing is all about.

In 1963, Ohio State University had some pretty strong feelings concerning how its beds were to be used. About as strong as my own. Merely bringing a woman into a men's dorm, for any reason, was a capital offense. This could cause both parties to be expelled from school and, judging by what I had seen of the place, possibly condemned to hell by burning at the stake. I had to be careful. The only person to receive even the slightest hint of my plan was Bill Tiffin. Since he had totally given up speaking about the same time he gave up dressing, Bill would make a fairly safe confidant. Still, all I told him was that if he ever returned to our room and found a handkerchief tied to the doorknob, not to come in. I did not think that this was too big of a thing to ask. Not when you considered how much my roommate used the room for his own purposes, such as they were. I really worked with Bill on this. Crouching down low, gently taking hold of his polishing hand, I repeated my instructions over and over. If you see a handkerchief, I told him, go milk a cow or take a nice march around the drill field. *But do not come in the room!* Finally, Bill Tiffin nodded his bill toward me. I was certain that I had gotten through.

Conditions looked perfect on the Sunday afternoon that I took Susan up to my room. Bill had left early in a cloud of Jade East. All the jocks and most of the other sorry-ass undersexed residents of Stanley Hall were off again at one of their pep rallies. No wonder these people lacked the energy for more important things. Andrew and the rest of his kind were surely out somewhere preaching or praying. The dormitory was nearly deserted.

Susan and I walked right up the back stairs and into my room like we were at the Holiday Inn. It was amazingly easy, but it was still exciting. You just cannot beat doing what you are not supposed to be doing for getting the blood up. Mine was up and flowing to all the appropriate places. While Susan undressed, something she could do faster than anyone I had ever met, I hung my handkerchief on the outside doorknob. I locked the door then wedged a chair beneath the inner knob just to heighten the sense of danger. My heart was racing. Even

Susan, who seemed to take about everything in stride, had become unusually aroused. I remember the quiet of that building right then. It was wonderful. I heard only my pounding heart and the muffled sound of far-off cheering.

Susan was radiant. Her long blond hair, free of leaves and twigs, fanned out luxuriantly over the pillow. Making love to her in my own bed would be every bit as magical as I had imagined. The only problem with sex in bed was that it was maybe *too* comfortable because Susan and I sure spent a long time on the preliminaries. In the bushes you tend to get down to business quickly. Even our special spot at Echo Lake was too damp and lumpy for encounters of the slow, lingering variety. Now we had entered a whole new erotic world. I figured that we did not have much time to spare, but I wanted to explore that world thoroughly. It was important that we did this thing, but it was also important that we did it right. Like losing your virginity in general, you only got to do this once.

That plain old dormitory bed transformed me from an animal into a sultan. I do not know how long Susan and I entertained each other with subtle new pleasures, but I suspect that it was longer than I thought. Maybe quite a bit longer. Anyway, we were finally getting close to consummating the new landmark in my sex life when I heard a faint tapping at the door. I froze. More tapping. "Come back later," I shouted. Susan sat up with a start. "What is it?" she whispered. "Probably just one of the maids who won't come in here during the week," I told her. We both listened as the tapping continued. It was weak but persistent. "Come back later—you can't come in now!" I shouted toward the door. The tapping got louder. Then a lot louder. I went over to the door as the tapping turned to knocking. Momentarily stunned, the image of Christ at the U.N. shot through my head. The knocking became pounding. Behind the pounding I could just barely hear a thin, wailing sound. The wailing grew in volume. Now I was able to make out some words that accompanied the sound—*rot-see, special drill meet, uniform.* The voice was one that I had seldom heard, but I instantly recognized it. If you heard it even once, there could be no mistaking the creaky, peeping, pissing-in-a-tin-cup voice of my roommate, Bill Tiffin. "Go away!" I shouted. "Don't you remember what I told you?" But the pounding and wailing went on. The man sounded like he was having some kind of a fit. There were other voices out in the hall now, which was beginning to alarm me. I ran back to Susan and told her to get dressed. We both raced to put our clothes on, but Susan, unfortunately, lacked the speed in this procedure that she possessed in its reverse. She was just buttoning her blouse when I heard a key enter the lock. The voices outside had grown considerably and ringing above them all was the perfect baritone of Andrew Ferguson. I simply could not believe that this was happening. Door strained against chair. Andrew summoned the names of his sainted ancestors. "Get under the bed!" I told Susan, but it was too late. Andrew hit the door with as fine a cross-body roll block as I had seen executed on any football field. It sent the chair flying and there we were. Andrew, Susan, and I just stood looking at each other— while Bill Tiffin walked calmly into the room, took his R.O.T.C. uniform from the closet, and left without so much as ever raising his hair-bill. Andrew returned to the hall and informed the craning, jostling mob of students that he had everything under control. He came back inside, slamming the door.

Happily, chivalry was included in Andrew's long list of manly virtues. He would deal with me personally and leave Susan to God. I was not sure who got the worse of that arrangement. For the moment, he instructed me to quietly sneak Susan back out of the building by whatever way I had brought her in. Keeping Stanley Hall free of scandal would temporarily take precedence over my own fate. This did not keep Andrew from launching into a frenzied assault on my character, full of dire warnings noted by Chapter and Verse. He slowed down only to catch his breath or occasionally reposition himself with respect to Susan who sat on my bed with her blouse still half-buttoned. When hellfire and damnation gave way to the proud Ferguson clan marching headlong into battle, I grabbed Susan and directed her toward the door. There was no way I could endure the Mother Scotland routine again. Besides, we had sinned enough already. I did not want to be responsible for giving Saint Andrew a stiff—- neck.

Susan and I stood outside the dormitory. It was one of those autumn days of pure blue and gold that will suddenly make central Ohio a match for anywhere in the world. Susan still looked good. She had weathered our ordeal in her usual calm fashion. The smell of Susan, mingled with the crisp, leafy breeze, did a lot to soothe my own spirits—and then some. I gave her this special little look, and she responded with her special little shrug. It truly was a shame to waste what was left of that fine afternoon. Arm in arm, we headed to Echo Lake for what I swore to the heavens would be our last bedless tryst. This was somewhat of an idle promise, but considering what I had just put Susan through, I figured she deserved at least that.

A fat harvest moon had just risen when I returned home to Stanley Hall—after a stop at the Rathskeller. Bill, of course, was in the room. Hard at it with a buffing brush, he never even looked up from the endlessly spit-shined shoes on his lap. It was all business as usual for Bill Tiffin. I was pleased to see him still wearing his R.O.T.C. pants and a T-shirt. At least my eyes would be spared the customary overexposure of ghastly, fish-belly white skin. My nose and lungs, however, were immediately assailed by what seemed a particularly strong dose of Shinola, Brasso, and cheap after-shave. How long had I been breathing that familiar, foul blend? I crossed the room and opened our one window. Looking back at Bill, a strange feeling came to me. How long had I been watching that same man, in that same position, polish that same pair of shoes? I looked at the window. And how long could I continue living with someone who had sabotaged the sacred event of my first ever bed sex?

I honestly cannot tell you what happened during the next several seconds. All I know is, I was suddenly at the window again and dangling Bill Tiffin out of it by his arms. Which is not really as awful as it might first sound. You see, there was a jog in the building that formed a flat roof between the sixth and seventh floors. By hanging halfway out the window myself, I was able to gently drop Bill onto that roof. Gently, but not too quickly. Like the act he had so rudely interrupted, this deserved to be done right. He just hung there, silent and dazed, while I unleashed my entire catalogue of grievances into that doughy, death's-head face, occasionally shaking his pitiful body for emphasis. When I was finally exhausted, I released him and shut the window.

Now, the word went around later that I had thrown my roommate out the window—and that, of course, is not true. There is a huge difference between throwing someone out of a seventh-story window and *lowering* him down to a perfectly safe roof. I would never throw anybody out of a window. Really.

I guess Bill must have stayed in shock for a while because the wailing did not come immediately. Once it began, though, it was really something. He got into it considerably better than he had earlier in the day, and there were some interesting new sounds, too. I enjoyed those sounds. I savored every hideous shriek. Okay, maybe Bill Tiffin could not help being the king of all geeks but even that was no excuse for committing a roommate's ultimate act of betrayal. Let the traitor scream. He could rot on the roof just as easily as he had been rotting in our room. What difference did it make? Like I have said, I was big on justice.

Andrew Ferguson charged into the room. "What the heck have you done now?" he shouted. I walked up to the man, pressing my face close to his. "I have arranged for a little privacy, *Andy*— that's what the *heck* I've done!" I stared right into his perfect blue eyes. "Speaking of which," I continued, "don't you ever knock?" Andrew held his ground. "Where is your roommate?" he demanded. "Aren't you in enough trouble already?" "He stepped out for some air, Andy," I replied. Close as we stood, Andrew and I shouted just to be heard over the noisy throng of students gathering at my door. Bill Tiffin's beautifully agonized cries faded in the distance. "You've been drinking!" Andrew announced. "That's right," I told him. "You should try it yourself sometime, Andy, it would do a lot to improve your personality—and I think there's a little something else you could use, too." Andrew puffed himself up to full Highland stature. "No Ferguson has ever touched alcohol!" "Screw your whole teetotalling, mutton-sucking, plaid-assed clan," I screeched. "If men in my family went running around in skirts I sure as hell wouldn't be bragging about it!" That really got things going: *Drunken sot! Bible-thumping parasite! Hellion! Pompous ass! Antichrist! Horny hypocrite! Fornicator! Prude! Hedonist! Dirty old man!...* Well, you get the idea.

A pair of hulking jocks finally escorted Bill Tiffin through the crowd and into our room. Presumably, they had hauled him inside by way of another window. Bill looked bad, even by his own unique standards. Pale to the point of transparency, shaking, whimpering, his hair-bill crumpled down in his face, my roommate staggered toward his bed and the comfort of a large flannel polishing rag. The R.O.T.C. shoes he had been shining still sat on the bed. I looked at Andrew, then I looked at those shoes. Andrew Ferguson and R.O.T.C.: God and Country— the twin pillars of Ohio's state-run bastion of higher education. I jumped away from Andrew, grabbed the shoes and flung them out the open window. A wail instantly went up from the bed.

"That does it!" shouted Andrew. "You are out of this dormitory! I want you to pack up your things and be out of here first thing in the morning."

I lunged back at Andrew but the jocks got between us. Patting my back, they gently restrained me and told me to take it easy. I was surprised at their new respect. These two had never cared much for me before, possibly because of the rumor that I was a communist. I guessed they figured that anyone who threw, or even lowered, a person out a window could not be all bad. "That's too long to wait," I shouted at Andrew. "I'm not spending another night in this goddamn prison!" "So be it!" thundered Andrew, crossing his arms over his chest just like a ham actor in one of those awful Bible movies that were so popular at the time. I began gathering up my belongings while Bill Tiffin curled into a fetal ball, clutching his polishing rag. And that was that.

So, here I am, in this fetid Vietnamese rice paddy. Andrew, true to Christian form, had me thrown out of school for bringing Susan into the dormitory. This swift and efficient execution of his moral duty did not go unnoticed by my draft board. The patriotic trustees of O.S.U. made sure of that. I was also officially blamed for Bill Tiffin's nervous breakdown. He left Stanley Hall the day after I did, and returned to his tranquil family farm to convalesce. Fine. I am paying for my sins. The avenging spirits of Fraternity, Propriety, Academia, and for all I know, Military Science, have all been appeased.

Lying in the muck, I think about the days when I lived with Holsteins on the wall and Brut in the air. I wanted justice, and this is where it's gotten me. Life has finally presented me with a situation that I can't write my way out of with some phony English essays. This, I have come to learn, will generally be the case. But if I ever do get out of here, I've promised myself that I'll become a real writer. I'll write about all I've been through, and Bill Tiffin will certainly be a part of it. Bill and I. We really hit the jackpot.

Adolph Hitler steps onto the porch of a small, tidy chalet. A tall man with white hair rises from a canvas chair to greet him.

"Adolph, how are you? Pull up a chair."

"Green vegetables. I've decided that green vegetables are the answer."

"Yes, greens are very important."

"No more bread, beans, cauliflower, potatoes—nothing but fresh, glorious greens."

"Just greens? Sounds a bit drastic, Adolph. Could cause gastric problems, trouble with the nervous system."

"No! I've already started the new diet, and I feel more strength and spirit than ever before in my life. We'll leave the starches for those pasty Frenchmen and thick Slavs."

"Carbohydrates are necessary."

"And no more fruit, either. Out with the Southern invaders! Oranges, lemons, tomatoes—tart little whores seducing the palate and poisoning the blood. No more! Only the harvest of German Soil can produce Pure German Blood."

"You know, I've never really agreed with that approach. I feel that some of the foreign foods could be very beneficial to the vegetarian diet: the peanut, banana—"

"Banana? BANANA! Just thinking about a banana makes me SICK! The word itself is disgusting: *ba—na—na*. BABY TALK! Not proper food for a soldier. Merely handling one is indecent, unmanly. The True German will learn to shun these unwholesome foods of the Southern perverts."

"And what about our German fruits?"

"THERE ARE NONE! Fruit is not German—it's just another part of the Southern contamination that threatens the will of our people."

"Apples?"

"Where there's fruit, there's wine, and where there's wine, you have the dull-witted Southern homosexuals good for nothing but stuffing their faces with dough and putrid cheese and dead flesh and fondling their BA—NA—NAS WHILE GERMAN SOLDIERS SHAPE THE DESTINY OF THE ENTIRE WORLD!"

Hitler gets up and walks to the edge of the porch where he stares vacantly at the countryside.

"You shouldn't get so excited, Adolph. It isn't healthy."

"The cabbage!" Hitler whirls around. "Aryan of the vegetable kingdom, staple of German Muscle and Blood. Good strong cabbage, lettuce, chard, spinach, cress—these will be the raw materials of the New German, pure in body and mind, grazing like a mighty stallion on wild sweet plants while the sullen beasts around him forever broken to the trough and feedbag bloat on the poisonous fodder of their decadent—"

"Adolph! Adolph! Come sit down again and tell me just how long you've been on this new diet."

Hitler begins pacing aimlessly around the porch.

"Green—the color of spring, rebirth, the blossoming of the New Germany. Germany's future, Germany's BLOOD WILL BE GREEN!"

"I think your new diet is causing a strain."

"NEVER! Just as Germany is strong enough for a Hitler, Hitler is strong enough for the New Diet."

"My God, you're not a ruminant—you can't live on grass."

"The New German *will* be able to live on grass if necessary—and wage war on grass. When our starving, miserable enemies see German soldiers contentedly grazing on their land they'll lose whatever heart they had for battle in a hurry!"

"Something else is troubling you, Adolph."

"They say he demands fresh meat three times a day. Rare, dripping."

"Who?"

"That malt-minded, blood-swilling, fornicating—"

The man walks toward Hitler to confront him directly.

"Who are you talking about?"

"Churchill, of course. He wants a meeting. He wants to get me alone with his fat jowls and that horrible turd-prick which is probably the only vegetable that ever enters his mouth, and of course we'll have to have a good old English meal of good old English roast beef—and braised bangers and basted bloaters and kippered kidneys and jugged giblets and pressed heifer and jerked hoofer and brain of boar and joint of neat and rack of beast and RAMEKINS OF FATTED STAG SHANK AND RASHERS OF SCUPPERED MUTTON SCRAPPLE AND FERKINS OF FETID FOX FLANK AND YAAAAAAAAAA...."

Hitler throws himself down on the porch deck and begins chewing on a plank. His mentor kneels beside him.

"Adolph, you're not a cow, but you're not a termite either. Now stop that!"

The Führer sits up and clasps his knees.

"And of course there'll be liquor. Gallons of beer, wine, whiskey, fermented blood to wash down the rest of the gore."

"You needn't be so *afraid* of meat. Eating meat is bad, of course, but you go too far."

"I'm not afraid of meat. I'm not. I'm not afraid of him. I'm not afraid of anything. WOMEN! THAT'S WHAT HE'LL DO—HE'LL BRING WOMEN. HE'LL TRY TO GET ME IN BED WITH ONE OF THOSE THICK-LIPPED, BIG-BOSOMED, RUMP-ROASTED ENGLISH WHORES! THEY'LL TAKE PICTURES. HE'LL TRY TO RUIN ME WITH WOMEN!"

The old man pats Hitler on top of the head.

"Don't worry, Adolph. Don't worry. I'm going to get you some bread and cheese. You need nourishment. You can meet with Churchill—you can handle him."

"Of course I'll meet with him. No, I can't. I will. I won't. I will I won't I…. WE'LL BLOW THAT TWEED-TRIMMED SLAUGHTERHOUSE RIGHT OUT OF THE ATLANTIC!"

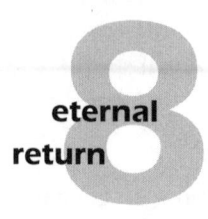

**eternal
return**

Sheila stared across the dinner leftovers at Carl.

"How about running that by me one more time, please."

"Sure." Carl plucked a cucumber slice out of a big wooden salad bowl. "It's really pretty simple. Scientists claim that matter can never be created nor destroyed—the atoms that make up things are always changing around into new combinations, but it's still the same old atoms. Right?"

"Okay."

"And everyone seems to agree that time is endless. So, given an infinite amount of time, every possible combination of atoms will eventually have to occur—and over and over again. Just like shaking the same dice forever in a huge cup."

"So that's why someday we'll be sitting here again just like we are right now?"

"Sure. It's an unavoidable consequence of having infinite time and finite stuff. But what's really interesting about this is that one day we'll be sitting here again and everything will be the same except this salt shaker will be over here." Carl slid the salt shaker a few inches across the table. "And the carpet will be red instead of blue. And some guy in China won't have a wart on his nose, and a beach somewhere will have one less grain of sand."

"All that could really happen?"

"It *has* to happen—if you accept the original premise of limitless time and limited atoms." Carl pulled some cold linguini from a bowl with his fingers. He dredged the noodles through a pot of sauce then dangled them over his mouth.

Sheila watched Carl as he sucked the linguini down with a slurp. She grabbed the bottle of Cabernet and filled her half-full wine glass to the top. "So this is what you philosophers talk about all day over at the university?"

"No, it's only one idea—mostly it's just something to make you think."

Carl and Sheila stared at each other.

"So," Sheila lowered her eyes and stroked the stem of her glass, "maybe like a zillion years from now we could be sitting here like this, but you'll be the one working your ass off every-day, and I'll be hanging around with all these genius professors talking about atoms and salt shakers and Chinamen?"

"That's right." Carl stared at Sheila until she lifted her head and their eyes met again.

"Well, it's nice to have something to look forward to."

"Hey, I've told you—if you want to quit your job, just quit it. We'll get by."

"On your salary? You hardly make enough to even pay the rent."

"I'm not going to be a teaching assistant forever...." Carl suddenly paused. If what he had been saying about time and matter were true, he would be a teaching assistant forever—with some rather lengthy gaps while his recombined atoms pursued other occupations. Carl's hand absently felt its way into the linguini bowl again. "In a few, years I'll be a full pro-fessor. We'll have security, money in the bank."

Sheila took a gulp of wine. "Maybe someday we'll be sitting here again just like this, but you'll eat dinner like normal people instead of waiting until we're done and then picking at everything that's left with your hands."

"That' right—I'll eat like 'normal' people, and maybe the salt shaker will have legs and be wherever it wants, and maybe the carpet will be unicorn fur, and maybe all of China will be one gigantic wart, and maybe beaches will be made of Parmesan cheese, and just maybe you won't drink so much wine that you have to start the same stupid argument all over again." Carl wiped sauce off his chin with the back of his hand

"Oh, the only problem is me drinking too much wine. It's because I drink too much wine that I work in a supermarket like some kid while you sit on your ass all day with these precious people who've never lifted anything heavier than a book in their precious lives. And then, I get to come home and watch you eat like an animal—with all that goddamn hair sticking out your nose."

Carl swiped a finger past his nostrils. Nose hair? Sheila had never mentioned his nose hair before. "Well, you better get used to it, because you're going to be watching it forever."

Carl attacked the salad bowl.

Sheila drained her wine.

"And I get to spend the evening with a wino." Carl watched Sheila as she filled her glass again.

"Maybe the next time we're back here, my atoms will be so scrambled up that I'll be Carol Franklin. Carol Franklin would never drink too much wine—Carol Franklin would never do *anything* wrong."

"I don't give a damn about Carol Franklin."

"You sure could have fooled me at that party Saturday."

"Look, we were talking shop—that's what people do at faculty parties."

"While I sit staring at the wall."

"Pouring down one drink after another."

"I was bored. I mean, what am I supposed to do, go up to some professor and tell him about the price of radishes or ask him what his philosophy is on canned soup?"

"You could have made a little more of an effort."

"Well, I'm really sorry. Maybe one of these times when I'm your wife again, I'll be smart enough to go to a philosophy department party without embarrassing you."

"I didn't say you embarrassed me."

"Of course not—you acted like I wasn't there."

Carl wound a strand of linguini around his index finger. He swooped it through the puddle of dressing at the bottom of the salad bowl, hooking the last tomato wedge with his thumb.

"Maybe the next time we're married, and we go to a party together, Carol Franklin will have that Chinaman's wart on her nose. I can't wait for that!'

Carl licked his fingers. "Look, Sheila—there isn't going to be a next time. That business about being back here again is just a mind game. Nobody really believes it."

Sheila shook the dregs of the wine bottle into her glass. "*I* believe it. It's the first thing I've heard in all your philosophy crap that makes any sense."

"Well, if it makes you feel better, fine—believe it."

"You bet it makes me feel better. It makes me feel wonderful thinking about how one day you and Carol Franklin will be working together trimming rotten cabbages and hauling around week-old fish while I sit on my ass in some classroom. You'll make a lovely couple, too—Mr. Hairy Nose and Mrs. Wart Nose."

Carl pushed his plate out of the way. He grabbed the bowl of linguini and banged it down in front of him. The concept of eternal return was just a trivial mental exercise, something to stimulate the mind toward genuine philosophical contemplation. Why did everything he mentioned to Sheila, lately, get so screwed up? Maybe it was eternal return, truly in action. That would certainly explain her wide range of unexpected behavior.

"…and I'll just be sitting there—"

"Well if your ass continues growing the way it has in *this* lifetime, you'll be prepared for it!" Bits of dry linguini noodle flew from the corners of Carl's mouth. "That thing's wider every time I look at it!"

"Oh, pardon me! I'll make sure the next time we're here that my ass atoms are arranged just the way you want them—that's something I really care about!"

"The next trillion times we're here, I won't even know you, and that'll be just fine with me!"

Sheila chugged the last of her wine. She grabbed the empty bottle and upended it over her glass.

"What are you going to do, squeeze it?"

Sheila pounded the bottle neck right through the glass. Carl shielded himself with a handful of clammy linguini noodles.

"Shit!" Carl slammed the linguini back into the bowl.

"The next time I come back here, I'm going to marry a bricklayer, and he'll love me no matter what, and I'll drink wine until I have to turn sideways to get through the door, and I hope you're a cockroach on the floor, so you can see how happy we'll be." Sheila threw her chair back and ran from the room.

"Why wait? You can start shopping around at construction sites tomorrow for all I care!" Carl poured the pot of sauce over the linguini. He looped a thick, dripping clot of pasta over his finger and pulled it up toward his mouth, wondering if it were really possible to live with another person. Well, he'd have all eternity to get it right.

moose

It's cold. Sixty-five-below-zero cold. Of course, when you look at the Big Picture, that's downright toasty. Out in space, and that's mostly what you got in the universe, just plain space, it's always about four hundred below. Also, if I may be morbid for just a minute, I figure that most of the people who ever lived in our particular neck of the universe are presently dead and here I am alive. So, looking at the Big Picture, I really can't complain.

Looking at the Big Picture has always been my problem. Looking at the Big Picture is why I'm sitting in a log cabin outside Fort Yukon, Alaska, sticking logs in a woodstove while the kids I went to school with are now sitting in half-million dollar homes sticking new programs in their computers. But what's the difference between a cabin and a mansion to a sun going super nova? What's the difference between a computer and a shovel to the lizards or bugs that usually rule this little planet? And how important are all those important ex-class-mates of mine going to be ten thousand years from now? The Big Picture. I think you can see my problem.

At sixty-five below zero, the world can start getting strange. Things that should be gases want to be liquids, liquids want to be solids, and your solids will bust up on you if you just look at them wrong. Nothing's happy anymore the way it is. This is all because of something called Entropy. Entropy means that it is the natural way of things to be as useless as possible. The colder the weather the more Entropy you get. And if you want to see how strong this Entropy is, try making it go backwards. Take a bucket of snow and try turning it into something useful like a bucket of water. You probably think you just put the bucket of snow up on the stove and in a few minutes you got a bucket of water, right? Well, you try that sometime and let me know how you do. Entropy.

So how come I know about Entropy and space and stuff like that? Got it all from the *Scientific American*. I used to be hell on those *Scientific American*s. See, I had this partner named Ivor who was the biggest, dumbest squarehead that ever packed a wad of snoose. I guess that's why every Christmas his mother sent him a subscription to *Scientific American*. Trying to improve his mind. Although from what I could see of Ivor's reading habits, she would have done better to send him a subscription to GI Joe Comics or maybe a lingerie catalogue. Anyway, Ivor passed the magazines on to me, and I have stacks of them. I couldn't understand half of what I read at first, but the same stuff will start coming around again and again, and pretty soon some things just start sticking with you. But that's not what got me thinking about the Big Picture. I just kind of naturally always had that in me. Then I stopped getting them, the magazines, when Ivor dropped through a hole in the ice. I checked, but I guess his mother must have canceled his subscription. That was about the cleanest way to leave this world you could ever want. One minute old Ivor is standing there, and then he's just gone. Disappeared. All we ever found was this big dribble of Copenhagen on the snow. Poor Ivor. Now that he's dead, I'm sure what he misses most is that damn snoose.

People will tell you that I lack ambition, and maybe it's true. Personally, I think I was born with an extra dose of Entropy. A mistake, sort of like having a tail or six toes. Now you combine that with a natural tendency to look at the Big Picture, and you don't exactly come up with someone who's going to be dean of Harvard or corner the market on soybeans. Hell, I'll tell you straight off that I have no ambition. But what I *do* have is plenty of firewood, nine bottles of R&R, and twenty-four packages of Top Ramen noodles. That's what I have. And I have common sense. You see, I have had the common sense to put myself in the situation where I don't *need* any ambition. How much *ambition* you suppose it takes to keep warm and to eat and drink? That's right. Even fighting an Entropy problem, a man with common sense will get by. Okay, I'd be happier with more than nine bottles of R&R, but that situation is no fault of my own, and I can prove it. When I was at the store last time, the nine bottles of R&R was the only liquor they had. Ask them. I planned to come back for more but the snow came and then the cold. And if you think you're going to snowshoe fifteen miles and back at sixty-five below, then you know even less than I think you do.

R&R stands for Rich and Rare which is a blended Canadian whisky that I am partial to, and it's a good thing since it is the only liquor you can get around here lately and not even all you want. But we've been through that already. Besides, I have used the Scientific Method to determine that nine bottles of R&R is exactly the amount I really want. Nine bottles of whisky in my cabin, nine planets in my solar system. A coincidence? We'll see. Now, at twenty-five shots per bottle and nine bottles, that gives me two hundred and twenty-five shots which is a very special number because it is one of the few numbers with a nice neat Square Root. Square Roots are very important to the Scientific Method. If you don't believe me, just check out any issue of *Scientific American* you like. The square root of two hundred and twenty-five is fifteen. Okay, let's look at those nine planets. If you number them by distance from the sun, which is the way scientists do it, Mercury is planet number one, Venus is two, Earth three, Mars four, and so on, all the way out to Pluto which is so far away it didn't even use to be a planet. When you add these nine numbers up you get forty-five. Now take Earth's number, three, multiply it by fifteen, which is the Square Root of nine times twenty-five, and what do you get? *Forty-five.* That's what you get! The *signature* number for our solar system. So is this a coincidence? My age happens to be forty-five. That is a coincidence. But nine bottles of R&R? Now perhaps you will have a better idea of what can be gained by paying attention to the Big Picture!

Of course, I don't still have all nine bottles of whisky. I didn't spend that money just for something to decorate my cabin with, and it's not for unexpected guests, either, because I've never had one of those, and if I ever do, I expect he would have the courtesy to bring his own liquor and maybe some extra. The only other person who's ever been in this cabin is Ivor, and he was about as close to having no one else around as you can get. But I'd be surprised to see Ivor again. Being a follower of the Scientific Method, I don't believe in ghosts which is also why I'm not afraid of the dark, and it's a good thing because in case you haven't heard, right now it's dark almost all the time. Just a little light around noon which is when I usually go out to bust up some firewood. Then it's dark again. Too dark to read unless I use the lantern, but it's low on fuel and I'm saving it, the fuel, in case I might need the lantern later on even though I don't know what for. This is a good example of Deductive Reasoning which is what scientists call the common sense that I just naturally have. I don't know what I might need the lantern for, but I can *deductively reason* that when and if I do need it, the lantern won't do me much good without fuel. This is why I don't use the lantern. This is also why I have just thrown my bundles of *Scientific Americans* into the woodstove. All the goddamn magazines in the world without a light are about as useful as all the goddamn lanterns in the world without any fuel. See how things get to be *interconnected?* Oh, and in case you think burning those magazines was some kind of improper thing to do, some insult to the mind, I want you to know that I threw all my Swedish Nature Camp magazines into the stove, too. Hah! You won't catch me napping that easily. I don't need any light to cook those Jap noodles, and I don't even want any for eating them. My big flashlight gives me all the light I need when I play plumb-wad.

The temperature got up to forty below, but it's back to around sixty-five below again. There is a world between these temperatures, but of course you would know nothing about that, even though I'm sure you think you do. You think that after twenty below it's all the same, right? I know that's what you think. Well let me tell you something. At twenty below, you don't even need a parka. At thirty below, you do. At forty below, you have to cover your face. At fifty below, it's hard to breathe and there's this *crackle* in the air. At sixty below, the air is so heavy you can feel it pushing down on you and if a hare farts five miles away you can hear it. What's it like after that? If you're so smart, *you tell me!*

I set up for plumb-wad this morning. This is the game played with three empty R&R bottles, three wads of tin foil, and a plumb bob hung from the ridge beam of the cabin. You stand the bottles side by side on the floor with the tin-foil wads sitting on their tops, and the plumb bob hanging at just the right height so that if you pull it back and let it swing, it will knock off the wads but just miss the bottle tops. When the wad goes off the bottle, it makes a nice sound, like putting your lips together and then blowing them apart. If you just knock off the middle wad, this is called a single-wad: one point. If you swing past it and knock it off coming back, that's a single-reverse-wad: two points. If you hit the left-hand wad going, the middle wad coming back, and the right-hand wad going again, that's a forward-N-wad and you get three points. These are the simple moves. A triple-reverse-'round-the-world takes lots of practice but it scores ten points. The idea of the game is to see how fast you can get to one hundred. Also, there is a lot of science in the way the plumb bob moves. Something hanging like that will even have your Conservation of Rational Momentum, which I have been so partial to after I saw it in one of the *Scientific Americans* that I memorized the term, and it's a good thing since the magazines are gone now. This is a very important term, and it has more Square Roots to it than a bear has dingleberries. Oh, did I forget to tell you? If you miss any one of the moves, its points are *deducted* from your score. Now I think you can see that this is not the silly, wimpy, faggy game you might have thought.

I saw him today when I went out for firewood. He was a big one. I didn't know they got quite that big.

I decided to use up that little bit of maple syrup I've been saving. When we were kids back in Wisconsin, we'd mix fresh maple syrup with snow. That was the way we liked it best. Now the whole world is snow, but since I am older and have common sense, I put the syrup on my noodles, and even though this was not so great, I figured that it was better than the eyeballs and octopus legs and other slime they put on those noodles in China. At trapping camp, Ivor would make pancakes all the time. He'd make them three times a day—he didn't care. I asked him once why if we were going to eat all those goddamn pancakes he couldn't put some blueberries or something in them. Next time he made pancakes they were full of little lumps and when I cut into mine there were all these peas. Canned green peas. I never complained about his pancakes again. Once when we were in a bar, Ivor said he could lay out ten pennies on his stiff dick. Some guy says right away that he can put ten cents on his own and then another ten. Ivor told the guy, Bullshit! but then the guy slaps these two dimes down on the bar, and everyone in there is laughing except Ivor. Finally, Ivor got to laughing himself, but then everyone else quit because sometimes Ivor had this way of laughing that wasn't really so funny. When you mix fresh maple syrup in with snow you get this sort of sweet slush that is better than any candy in the whole world.

Fifteen feet to the top of his antlers and staring right at me. Perfectly still. Could have been stuffed. I watched from the cabin door. He walked away without looking back.

Now that I have five empty R&R bottles, plumb-wad has become a lot more...*part of the Big Picture.*

He came again today. Never would have known he was there if I hadn't opened the door. Twenty feet from the ground to his chin beard and looking me straight in the eye. I waved. He wasn't interested.

Did I ever tell you about the time we were fishing on the Kobuk River, Ivor and me? It was warm and there was wind enough to keep the bugs down, so we slept out right by the river. In the middle of the night, I woke up because Ivor was making these funny noises in his sleep, giggling kind of. I thought maybe he'd chewed some amanitas or something, but there's also this smell like motor oil and shit and then I see this big black lump which is a bear with its big bear rump sticking up in the air and its mouth down licking Ivor's feet. You never can tell what a bear will do. Once I was camping alone, and when I got up in the morning there was this bear curled up sleeping right next to my tent. Like he was lonesome or something. Then for no reason at all, when you least expect it, one will come charging out at you like some halibut fisherman who's been mixing schnapps and wine. Anyway, I chased the bear off of Ivor and he never even knew about it. Slept right through the whole thing with this big silly grin on his face. That bear could have just as easily tore his leg off, but Ivor was always lucky that way. He could fall into a barrel of assholes and come out with a tit. But then he fell through that hole in the ice and didn't come out at all. Now I know you think I'm making this up, about the bears and all, but I'm finally going to just have to tell you that I don't really give a shit what you think. *There!* You think the only things that ever happened are what you read about in books. That's what you think. Well, some day *I'm* going to write a book. I'm going to call it "Everything in the World I Don't Give a Shit About" and it will be one of the longest, greatest books ever written and there will be a whole chapter on "What You Think"!

Stepped out for a chunk of firewood today and noticed a strange shadow on the front of the cabin. He was standing broadside twenty yards away. Rigid as a show dog. Not a wiggle of the hide or shift of a hoof. I could have walked under his belly with five feet to spare.

There was only one time when the *Scientific American* let me down. That was the article on dredging rivers and canals. I think they were a little off on that one because how can digging out the bottom of a river make it deeper when the whole river is just going to drop down into the new bed? That's just common sense. All you're going to get is the same river with higher banks. I've been meaning to write them about it, and I even made some drawings, but now I've decided to let the whole thing go because everything else they wrote about was so good, and also I don't like to come on like some kind of a wise-ass. I figure anyone's bound to slip up once in a while. But I still think about that river, and I'm sure I'm right. I'm sure of it.

I am beginning to like this moose. I have named him Sir Isaac after the man who invented gravity.

Finally completed an eight-wad-Lucky-Pierre. Twenty points. This is where I set the plumb bob swinging in a big circle around all the bottles and when it gets running low on Rational Momentum it starts picking off the wads one at a time from the end wads to the ones in the middle. I help by making the spaces between the bottles not all the same. With the bottles and the spaces between them there are fifteen places for the plumb bob to go. Fifteen is the number that connects whisky bottles and the planets. Remember? Scientists call this number a Constant because it never changes, and this is good because if things in science kept changing it would be hard to get a look at the Big Picture which is what scientists are always trying to do even though I just do it naturally. Constants are about as important in science as Square Roots, and I have memorized some of them. Planck's Constant: 6.24. Pi: 3.141592. C: 186,282. What's fun is to pretend the wads are people and the plumb bob is God. Sometimes the plumb bob will *jump* when you don't expect it and hit a wad that you'd swear it was going to miss. This is a beautiful thing to see. As beautiful as that little bit of noonday sun shining through my last bottle of whisky or a man falling through a hole in the ice.

At first, I thought he wasn't there today, but only because the space between his legs and under his belly was so big. His bulk just floated above the birches…. *Does anyone else know about this?*

Do you?

10

sam's habit

Karen walked briskly into the house and threw her purse down on the couch. Sam was at the kitchen table reading the newspaper.

"Well," said Karen, "I guess I've got things smoothed over with the Alexanders. At least they won't be suing us."

"Good."

"Of course we can forget about ever getting another invitation from them or any of their friends."

"Also good."

"Look, they've been very reasonable about this thing. Some professor from the university looked at it and he thinks it might be able to bloom again."

"Wonderful." Sam leafed through his newspaper without reading anything.

"After all these times, I still don't believe it. A hybrid that was named for her great-grandfather—and in front of all those people."

"You know I can't help myself."

"That beautiful flower."

"Oh, 'beautiful flower' my ass." Sam finally looked up from the paper. "The only reason she brings that silly thing out is to have an excuse to start bragging about her wonderful ancestry."

"Some people are proud of their families, Sam."

"Yes, she comes from a 'very old family'—just like everyone else in the whole goddamn world. You know, the only thing the Bible-thumpers and the evolution people agree on is that all of our families have to be exactly the same age. Was her family here before Adam and Eve? Does she have documented proof that one of her ancestors swung out of a tree before one of mine did?"

"That's not what she means."

"I know perfectly well what she means. By the way, that orchid tasted awful."

"Really? Not as appetizing as that wine you drank from the bucket everyone was spitting in at the wine-tasting party?"

"That actually didn't taste too bad."

"People got sick from that one. They were in the bathrooms retching."

"They were a bunch of phonies, just like the crowd at the Alexanders'. I think maybe that's why I do it—it's a form of protest."

"How about the time you insisted that we go watch that faith healer, and you swallowed the tumor he pulled out of the deaf man's ear. What were you protesting there—common sense? Those rednecks were going to kill you."

"The 'tumor' was a piece of hamburger. I recognized it right away. And those people weren't about to kill anyone—they were too scared. They thought I was the devil."

"Maybe they were right. You're sick, Sam, and I can't take much more of it. You need to see a doctor."

"The best part of that whole thing was that the preacher and his 'deaf' sidekick were laughing. Those crooks thought it was *funny*." Sam got up from the table and began pacing around the room. "The son of a bitch actually winked at me. Here's these yokels running around shrieking and covering their children's eyes, and he's up there enjoying the show."

"We were lucky to get out of there alive, and you know it. If you don't do something about this, Sam, someday it really *will* get you killed." Karen slumped down into a chair. She was starting to cry. Sam continued to pace.

"Sometimes it's the best way to make a point."

"What was the *point* in eating that piece of preserved wedding cake from my grandmother's wedding?"

Sam stopped pacing and looked down at Karen. "I don't know what happens to me. I just can't help myself."

"That was her most cherished possession in the whole world. Now I don't feel comfortable around my own grandmother anymore—she thinks I married a lunatic. And what about that time with the funeral wreath? People were fainting."

"I just can't control it, Karen. Really."

"And the prize cucumber at the state fair, and those rare tropical fish, and...."

11

city

Jerry and Bud sat in the park tearing open brown paper lunch sacks.

"All right!" said Jerry, placing half a sandwich in front of Bud. "Roast beef."

"My oh my, ham on rye." Bud handed Jerry half of a ham sandwich with lettuce and mayo.

The men greedily unwrapped each sandwich, tossing the peanut-butter-and-jellies into a trash barrel along with the Oreos, Fig Newtons, and carrot strips. Baby food. These were grown men with serious appetites.

"Tuna!"

"Keep the whole thing, Jerry—I'm sick of tuna."

"You sure?"

"Yep... My God, what kind of crap are people feeding their children these days?" Bud opened a sandwich, revealing an odd-smelling green paste.

"What is it?"

"I don't know."

"Shit-can it—we got plenty of good stuff."

Jerry was the one who had come up with the idea of stealing the school kids' lunches. It was easy. You just went to a playground about ten minutes before the morning bell and gathered the sacks while the kids were absorbed in their basketball, hopscotch, or whatever. The more sacks you took, the better chance you had for a decent meal. This was a poor part of the city and some of the lunches were pretty meager.

The men stretched out on the lawn after they ate. Bud reached into his shirt pocket and dumped out a pile of cigarette butts. It was Bud's job to collect the butts while Jerry stole the lunches. Jerry knew that Bud stashed the choicest butts for himself in another pocket but he didn't care. Sometimes he ate a sandwich on his way to the park.

■ ■ ■

It was sunset when Jerry and Bud met up in the park again. Grinning proudly, Bud waved a ten dollar bill.

"Where'd that come from?" asked Jerry, suspiciously.

"I found it."

Jerry stared at Bud. "You *found* it?"

"I was at the Trailways station looking for butts, and I found it on the floor."

Jerry kept staring at Bud. He knew that the sort of people who passed through the Trailways station were not likely to misplace a ten-spot. Also, he knew that Bud was capable of an occasional mugging when the circumstance presented itself. Jerry was a thief. He believed in stealing, and he was good at it. Mugging was something else. The trick was to live by your wits. Any brute could hit someone on the head and take his money.

"Really—it was just lying on the floor."

"Okay." Jerry softened his gaze. "Rose's?"

"Yeh, Rose's!"

■ ■ ■

Rose's Café was their favorite place. It was a tiny Chinese restaurant, a hole-in-the-wall you could walk by without ever noticing. Jerry liked the hand-painted sign in the window: CHINA FOOD HERE OR TO TAKE IT OUT. He knew that when it came to restaurants, a bad sign was a good sign. Poor English meant that the proprietors were new arrivals who still cooked for the public the way they cooked for themselves back home. It took most immigrants a while to learn how to cut corners and start making a profit.

Jerry and Bud were the only customers in the restaurant. They sat in one of its four cramped booths. Rose's husband, an old wisp of a man who was both cashier and sole waiter, shuffled over from his station by the door. Why, wondered Jerry, did all Chinese past a certain age appear to have such difficulty walking? The man took their order then relayed it in his own language to Rose, standing patiently by the kitchen door. In an instant, there was a loud sizzling sound. Jerry and Bud smiled. Whenever they came to Rose's they ordered the same thing: fried rice and barbecued pork. The men had nowhere to cook and mostly lived on the sack lunches and dumpster scraps, plus whatever small items Jerry could shoplift from the supermarkets. The mounds of steaming rice and succulent pork always seemed like a miracle.

■ ■ ■

Bud went in the basement window first. Jerry took their bedding out from the hiding place under a pile of rubble and stuffed it through the window. Bud helped Jerry lower himself down to the concrete floor. The basement was the boiler room for a high-rise apartment building. It was relatively free of rats, roaches, and other vermin, maybe because of the fuel oil fumes. And it was always warm. If they stayed away during the day and were careful to leave no signs of their presence, Jerry and Bud would be able to sleep there as long as they wanted. Jerry lay on his bedroll staring up at the maze of pipes overhead. He liked to think about all the apartments connected to the pipes and make up stories about the people who lived in them. That was a good way to fall asleep.

■ ■ ■

Jerry approached the school, one he had never visited before. He was attracted by the easy access to the playground. Playgrounds were becoming more and more like prison yards, but this one still had a broad gate open to the street. Jerry walked boldly through. A lifetime on city streets had taught him how to belong, how to disappear into any scene he entered. Even here, he would be unseen.

Inside the gate, Jerry walked with his eyes straight ahead. It was a raw, blustery morning, but the schoolyard was full of activity. The children seemed so loud and wild. Jerry remembered that it was Friday. He thought back to his own childhood and how long the school week could be for a restless ten-year-old. As usual, most of the lunches were lined up along one edge of the blacktop playing area. There were some lunch boxes mixed in with the paper sacks, but Jerry never took any of those. Swiftly, confidently, he began picking up the lunches and dropping them into his shopping bag. The children were making such a noise that he never heard the little girl walk up behind him.

"Hey! What you think you're doing?"

Jerry turned and looked down at the girl. She was only in the third or fourth grade, but she somehow had all the bearing of a grown woman. Jerry was fascinated by her. She made him feel as though suddenly *he* were a child.

A boy walked from the blacktop over to the strip of lawn where Jerry and the girl were standing. "What's going on here?"

"This old fart was stealing lunches."

"Oh yeh?" The boy was about twelve, tall and thin. Jerry could see that he had carefully groomed himself, from his shoes to his hair, to look as threatening as possible. He shot Jerry a perfect offhand sneer. Jerry stared at the kid. It was impossible to imagine a more totally insolent creature.

Jerry moved toward the gate. He dropped his shopping bag and started to run, but the boy had grabbed onto his coat. The girl threw herself at his legs. Suddenly, Jerry was on the ground with the girl on top of him. She punched wildly at his chest and head, spitting in his face between horrible shrieks of abuse: "Filthy old bastard! Pervert!"

"Fucking creep!" The boy hovered over them, kicking Jerry with his pointed boots.

Jerry lay frozen. He watched the woman-child through his raised arms, stunned less by her blows than the image of her incredible fury. Where had such anger come from? He remembered his grade-school sweetheart, Cheryl. They lived in the same building and played together every day. When they grew up, they were going to get married and have an apartment of their own. Children were not like that anymore. Children had changed. The city had changed.

Kids came swarming over to the excitement now, led by a boy with a baseball bat. Jerry had pushed the girl off of him and was almost on his feet when the side of his head went numb. His ear was on fire, and he could feel the trickle of blood. He had to move. He had to get out of there before the bat found him again, before the teachers came running out of the school. Kicking and flinging children, Jerry fought his way to the gate. He ran straight into the heart of the crowded street.

When Jerry was two blocks from the school with no one chasing him, he knew he was safe. The crowd, as always, had protected him. But now people in the crowd were staring at him. Jerry looked down at his torn, bloody clothes. More than anything else, Jerry hated to stand out. Attracting attention went against all of his instincts, all he had learned. He needed a refuge.

Jerry headed down a side street toward the new office building. The building had originally been a warehouse, and he knew that there was still a loading dock in the rear that he could crawl under and be completely hidden. He had often slept there in the past. Jerry moved through the crowd as quickly as he could without bringing more attention to himself. When he reached the loading dock, he made sure there was no one around, then slipped down into the shadows. He felt safe again. Crouched in the dark, Jerry pressed the sleeve of his coat against his torn ear. He had had a close call that morning, but mostly he kept thinking about that girl and the hatred in her eyes. The city was his whole world, but there was so much about it that he no longer understood. Jerry watched as occasionally a lone businessman or office worker walked past, taking the shortcut to a parking lot. They would get into their cars and drive off to their homes. These people had good lives, but most of them looked as vicious as the children he had fought off in the schoolyard. Jerry crouched in the dark watching them.

■ ■ ■

Jerry and Bud met that evening at their usual spot. Bud looked Jerry over.

"Hey, Jerry, what happened to your ear? You get in a fight?"

"Nah—it's nothing."

"You okay?"

"*Just forget it!*"

Bud had never seen Jerry in such a mood. He reached into his pocket and offered him a butt, one of the good ones.

Jerry pulled a fresh pack out of his coat. He held it out toward Bud.

"Good score," said Bud. "Where'd you get those?"

"I came into some money today."

"Oh yeh, how'd you do that?"

"Look—I got some money, *okay?*"

The men smoked their cigarettes without speaking. Suddenly Bud's face lit up. "Hey Jerry, Rose's?"

"No, we're not going to that dump anymore. Come on, we'll find someplace good."

"Sure." Bud shrugged and followed Jerry out of the park.

the new war 12

Colonel Stang stepped smartly into the war room.

"General Galbraith, sir, the initial sorties have been completed."

"Yes, and with what results, Colonel?"

"According to our VIP, sir, the mission was a total success."

" 'VIP'?"

"Virtual Impairment Projection, sir."

"Colonel Stang, will you please continue your report in plain American."

"Sir, I was only...."

"Busting my withered old balls with double talk. Wasn't there aerial reconnaissance? Do we have ground observers?"

"That information is currently being assessed by—"

"Colonel Stang, what the bloody hell did we drop on the enemy and what did it do to them?" Gen. Galbraith cradled his chin on both fists and hunched forward across his desktop. His famous jowls flared. The general was only months from retirement but his classic Marine-Corps-poster jawline was as square and fearsome as ever. He glared at the young colonel.

"Well, according to plan, we peppered the hillsides with toasters, fans, radios, and other small appliances, and hit the suburbs with water heaters, refrigerators, washers and dryers, and a few old VW bugs. Then we unleashed the '58 Buicks and Caddies right in the center of town—along with the used tires."

"Used tires? With the heavy ordnance?"

"Yes, sir. They have an extremely high Serial Elastic Aftershock Coefficient."

"In other words, they bounce."

"Yes, sir. They bounce."

"How many tires were dropped?"

"Two million, sir."

"Good, good, excellent.... Is that a lot of tires to drop on a city?"

"Yes, sir, I believe it is."

General Galbraith leaned back in his chair. How had this happened to him? After nearly half a century of involvement in conventional warfare he was now commanding the new president's policy of Constructive Destruction. The disgustingly young and energetic new president had promised a more "upbeat" means of dealing with the nation's enemies and now it was finally being employed. The strategy was simple. Waste dumps and landfills were bursting at the seams, so we would kill two annoying birds with one unwanted stone by bombarding persistent bad guys with our garbage and junk. Bombs were expensive. This stuff was free, plentiful, and in the way. The new method of warfare would help solve one of the country's biggest problems while immobilizing an enemy at the same time. When the capital of a belligerent nation was waist-deep in dead batteries, old tires, bedsprings, washing machines, and moldy cheese, even the most fanatical foe would surely yield. The junk could be sorted by size and destructive potential and used like conventional artillery. Also, junk-blitzing would save us from the expense of having to rehabilitate the countries we destroyed. Salvageable parts from all those broken appliances would be the raw material for new cottage industries, and the rest could be mixed with concrete to build cheap housing. A poor country that was trashed instead of bombed might end up being better off in the long run.

The general focused on Col. Stang again.

"How has morale been so far?"

"Generally very good, sir. We've had just a little problem over in Third Division, Army Air Corps—two men have applied for conscientious objector status."

"*What?*" General Galbraith pounded his antique oak desk. "That's a veteran combat unit. My God, if a man can drop a ton of dynamite on the enemy, surely he can drop a refrigerator on him!"

"That's exactly what we told them, sir."

"What's being done with these men?"

"We've begun processing them through the appropriate channels and—"

"Yes, yes, of course…. What about biologicals? Have any organic agents been employed?"

"That's outside my field, sir. Captain Holland is an expert in those matters and he's in the next room."

"Bring him in here, Stang."

Colonel Stang did an about-face and quick-stepped out of the room. He returned with Captain Holland. The two young officers stood before General Galbraith.

"Hammond—what organic substances were used in today's offensive?"

"Holland, sir. The Seventh Wing B-52 Tactical Air Command successfully discharged eighty full payloads of CHAFERS over the metropolitan area of the target city?"

"Chafers?"

"Yes, sir."

"What the hell is a *chafer?*"

"That's the basic Chunked And Formed Encapsulated Raw Sewage unit, sir."

The general tilted his head and squinted toward Captain Holland.

"Captain, perhaps you can inform me as to the exact nature of the raw sewage unit—I somehow do not recall a reference to this weapon in any arsenal I am acquainted with."

"Yes, sir. Raw sewage is molded into blocks which are contained by a thin plastic membrane and then frozen for easier handling. These units, CHAFERS, are loaded into B-52s and partially thawed en route to achieve a consistency that yields maximum coverage upon impact."

"What is a standard payload, Captain?"

"At fourteen pounds per CHAFER and a carrying capacity of six thousand units, that makes a standard payload of approximately ninety thousand pounds, sir."

"And the estimated casualties for such a payload is what?"

"This weapon system does not carry a lethal rating, sir. Its purpose is to mainly annoy the enemy... as the name might imply, sir."

"*Of course*, Captain. Of course!"

The general leaned back again and stroked his mighty mandibles. Eighty payloads at ninety thousand pounds each—yes, a capital splattered with four thousand tons of shit might be significantly annoying to the enemy.

General Galbraith prepared to continue his questioning but Captain Holland broke in again.

"We've been working on some heavier, more destructive sewage delivery systems but complaints have been coming from Geneva. I'm afraid we might be on hold until international guidelines can be drawn up."

"Damn!" The general thumped his old desk. "If it were up to those bleeding-heart socialists we wouldn't be able to drop stale marshmallows on the enemy."

"Yes, sir, that's true," said Captain Holland.

"Very true," said Colonel Stang.

"Okay, Hammond," General Galbraith nodded wearily toward the captain, "have you anything else to report on today's mission?"

"With respect to organic ordnance, sir, a sizeable amount of pork was also dropped today."

"Pork? Is that pork as in P-O-R-K," the general traced each letter in the air with his forefinger, "or pork as in a pig's ass?"

"A pig's ass, sir. Surplus meat along with waste products from several slaughterhouses."

"And to what end, Captain, do we drop pork on people?"

"It's strictly for the psychological effect, sir. This is really outside of my field but Lieutenant Colonel Nagy is in the other room. He is an expert in these matters and I would be happy to—"

General Galbraith waved the captain off. He picked up his phone and pushed a button. "Amanda, please send in Lieutenant Colonel Nagy. Thank you."

Lieutenant Colonel Nagy appeared instantly beside the other two officers. General Galbraith looked him over. Another trim, bright-eyed wiseass. He was about half the general's age and nearly a perfect clone of the disgustingly young and energetic new president. The general addressed him without returning his salute.

"Okay, Nagy, enlighten me about the purpose of today's pork drop, if you will."

"Yes, sir. The enemy is mostly Moslem, sir, and they consider pork extremely offensive."

"I see. Did we include sweet potatoes and cornbread in the bombardment?"

"No, sir. As with most pork raids, we accompanied the meat with pornography. It was pretty much a standard P and P."

"Pornography?"

"Moslems also find pornography very offensive, sir. Men

who are not permitted to view a woman's bare ankle become seriously unbalanced when their streets are carpeted with back issues of *Pink Pussycat Parade* and life-size centerfolds of 'Miss Bimbo Akimbo'. We have also been experimenting quite successfully with laser-guided X-rated videos."

"My God!" General Galbraith rose to his feet. "We used to level an enemy city to the ground—now we airlift in a catered stag party! How about some booze, Nagy? Maybe we should send in the booze, too. What the hell' s a party without something to drink?"

"Well… actually, sir, we've been working with the people over at Alcohol, Tobacco and Firearms and they've provided us with large quantities of confiscated moonshine to include in our raids. Alcohol is strictly taboo in the Moslem culture, sir."

"We drop liquor on these people?"

"Yes, sir. When dealing with a nation of teetotalers, alcohol can be a potent weapon. Peasants who collect our raw sewage for fertilizer will often run from a puddle of Scotch."

General Galbraith fell back into his chair and closed his eyes. The image of a giant martini shimmered up between them. Why didn't someone drop one of those on him, right now? A lifetime of service to his country and it would all end like this. The general contemplated the men in front of him. Where had the real officers gone? Where were Bulldog, Chesty, Vinegar Joe…?

The general's reverie was broken by his aide, Lieutenant Hansen, bursting into the room.

"General! Alpha base has been hit by a missile!"

General Galbraith just stared at the man. The three young officers were instantly milling about, all talking at once.

"*General!*" repeated Lieutenant Hansen.

"Yes, Hansen, yes. What kind of missile was it that struck the base?"

"It was apparently one of those clunky old hand-me-downs that the enemy's been getting from their Asian allies, sir."

"The heathens!" screamed Colonel Stang. "I'm sure it was just a lucky—"

"Shut up, Stang!" The general stared again at Lieutenant Hansen's dog-ugly face and bad haircut. At least the man looked like a soldier. Okay, what type of warhead are we talking about here, Hansen? Did it explode?"

"Yes... sort of, sir."

"*Sort of?* Hansen—did the warhead explode or didn't it?"

"Well..."

"Hansen! What exactly was the nature of this warhead?"

"It appears to have been a dead camel, sir. A very dead camel. And there was also..."

"We've been prepared for just this sort of retaliation," said Colonel Stang, stepping forward.

The general pounded his desk. "Shut up, Stang! And there was also *what*, Lieutenant Hansen?"

"There was this highly destructive incendiary material...."

"What type of incendiary material would that be, Hansen?"

"Well, sir, according to our analysis it appears to be about a fifty-fifty mixture of rancid hummus and couscous."

General Galbraith slumped back in his chair and closed his eyes again.

"It's hard to believe, General, but when this mixture is subjected to extremely high temperatures it turns into something similar to napalm."

The general massaged his gunmetal temples and flexed his celebrated jaw muscles.

"No," whispered General Galbraith, "I believe it. I'll believe anything you tell me."

13

sweet sunny south

Samantha and I lie on the beach. We are in the deepest possible South with its sneaky, brutal sun. This is not the sun I expected. I had pictured the big yellow ball in a child's drawing, the sun of a perfect sunny-side-up egg smiling down from the blue sky on honeysuckle, hummingbirds, and Uncle Remus. The Gulf sky is seldom blue. The sun is everywhere but unseen—hiding in the haze, working me over. I imagine that it is punishing me for being so awkward, for not knowing the local ways, the slow and easy style.

It is July, 1962, and I have just celebrated my birthday. I am now seventeen, a Yankee, and a semi-virgin. I thought it would be simple—one day you're a virgin and the next day you're not. My problem is that my first attempts at sex were so clumsy that I'm not sure they really counted. In a way, I hope they didn't. If my accomplishments in bed to this point were the real thing, then I figure the whole business is highly overrated. Still, a man is supposed to keep score. Nothing, it seems, is simple anymore.

I watch Samantha, perfectly still on her towel. The blasting heat does not bother her—it wouldn't dare. Samantha is a genuine Southern belle, and even the elements must show a proper respect. The guerrilla sun kneads and pounds my belly, tears the skin from my shoulders, but only touches the few golden hairs sparkling over Samantha's rich tan. There is a little moisture on her upper lip. I'm soaked. Belles, of course, know the secret to not sweating. It's part of the education—along with holding quarters in your armpits at the dinner table so you can't reach for what you should be served, or learning to smile right into the eyes of a man when he helps you in or out of a car to distract him from sneaking a look at your legs. Even a gentleman—belles associate only with gentlemen—will sometimes succumb to this temptation. Samantha has explained these things to me, and I am fascinated. I thought belles were just born that way. I know nothing. Samantha has also had lessons in music, posture, dancing, and even kissing. Kissing lessons? If Northern girls received such thorough training, I wouldn't be suffering with this uncertainty about the status of my manhood. Finally, I am in good hands.

■ ■ ■

We wheel into the Dixie Queen drive-in in my borrowed Lincoln Continental convertible. Pure class. The car belongs to Lucky, whose real name is Leon, a distant cousin I've been staying with. Relatives in the North had told me to look up Leon. No one knew anything about him, but he was blood, no matter how diluted, and I was assured that he would be hospitable. Lucky has turned out to be a gambler and minor hoodlum who wears silk suits and pointed, black and white shoes with wooden heels. I like Lucky. He's capable of making the big gesture, so tonight we have the Continental. Among the Continental's many amazing features is the ability of the front seat to fold completely backwards so that the car can be turned into a plush, open-air bed. This is done electrically, like raising and lowering the windows—you just push a button. Lucky has explained about the bed in great detail, and I promised him that I would put it to good use. Lucky is ten years older than me and very concerned about my sex life. It seems like all the older men who I meet are. Samantha loves the car. She sits close, right up against me. When I drove Lucky's Chevy, she never sat that close.

As soon as I park, Samantha removes the bubble gum from her mouth and places it in my hand. The first time I was confronted with this ritual, I was ready to jump on the next Greyhound heading north. I was devastated—figured that I had strayed too far, entered a territory too alien for my survival. Was this a local gesture of acceptance? Rejection? Was there a gum shortage? Did a proper gentleman periodically inspect a lady's bubble gum to make sure it was still fit for her to chew? Now, I'm perfectly at ease with the gum business. I actually enjoy it. According to Samantha, it's not ladylike, or bellelike, to dispose of one's own gum. This is a man's job and the whole thing must be handled discreetly and without fanfare. Holding the sweet, pink gum, still warm from Samantha's mouth, gives me a thrilling sensation of intimacy. I wait until she isn't looking—this is how it's done—and toss the gum out of the open convertible. True chivalry. I'm definitely making progress.

The carhop, a black boy in his early teens, attaches a tray and hands me the menu. Samantha will have a strawberry milkshake for her dinner. She eats nothing but sweets—ice cream, soft drinks, candy, pastry, and something she calls "French breakfast" which, for all I can tell, is coffee and a doughnut for twice the price you pay when it's called coffee and a doughnut. She drinks her coffee iced and with four spoonfuls of sugar. The closest thing to a real meal I have ever seen Samantha eat was a plate of grits which she smothered in honey, topped with raspberry preserves, and washed down with a Coca-Cola. I find that Samantha's unusual diet only enhances her magic. All of my life, I have been told that such eating habits would lead to ruin. Samantha's teeth, complexion, and figure are perfection. My own constitution is rooted in the north woods and the need to keep up with a body that continues growing each year. I order a hamburger, the biggest one they've got.

When our food arrives, Samantha is still sitting so close to me that her hair rests on my shoulder. She has the usual sweet fragrance about her. Since the smell persists when we go swimming, I assume that its source is something other than perfume. Perhaps it comes from her literally being made of sugar. It's a wonderful smell. Samantha drinks her shake with dainty, well-paced sips. Amazing. Those gross beasts I used to date up north would have had the whole thing finished already and be slurping around at the bottom of the cup. Samantha must be the only person in the world who can drink a milkshake without ever slurping.

My hamburger tastes awful. When I complain to Samantha, she gives me her best getting-out-of-the-car smile and tells me that I better eat it—I could be needing some extra energy later on. This is a little more than I am prepared for. I wonder if she picked up this sort of thing in her belle training. My guess is that she's improvising—pure Samantha and very effective. I resist, possibly for the first time in my life, the temptation to say something stupid, and I say nothing. The semi-virgin with no training at all is learning. I smile back. Samantha says that she knows the food isn't very good, but there is another reason why she has insisted that we come here. This is a very special restaurant. This is *the* place where dances come from. Dances? Not just this town, not just this neighborhood, but right in this drive-in is where all the new dances originate—The Pony, The Froog, The Watusi, The Boogaloo. Another of Samantha's surprises. She's caught me again. I have no idea what she's talking about—I can't even fake it. It's the carhops, Samantha informs me. You give them some money, and they dance for you. This is how the white teenagers learn to dance. She instructs me to give our carhop fifty cents. If I just throw the money in his direction, he'll know what to do. While I sort through some coins, Samantha suddenly bursts out with the information that she once danced with a Negro. It was at an after-hours bar and barbecue joint where people went to hear rhythm and blues music. Even in these final days of the Old South, the still officially segregated South, this is a bold confession. No doubt about it, she's really letting loose tonight. I've got it made. I figure that even belles must occasionally give in to their desires, and for this purpose I am very convenient. I'll be leaving at the end of the summer, but there's something else, too. Since I am not a gentleman, Southern or otherwise, a roll in the hay with me is like dancing with a Negro or like my bungled sexual adventures up north—it won't really count. I make a good show of appearing shocked at Samantha, which she enjoys, and toss two quarters onto the pavement with a sneer. Samantha presses tightly against me as the kid pockets the money and goes into his dance. He's good. He manages to move everything but his feet, the reverse of my own particular style. Well, this is the place where dances come from—it should be no surprise that it gets the best dancers. They probably have auditions. The carhop stares right at me with a big grin that says, "You couldn't do this if you tried for the rest of your life." True. I give him another sneer. With the radio turned on, loud, and Samantha nearly in my lap, we pull out of the restaurant in grand style. Lucky would be proud of me.

■ ■ ■

The drive-in movie is immediately a setback. An Elvis Presley triple feature. Five hours of Elvis facing me, and I have the worst case of gas in history. Even in a convertible, gas at the drive-in has to be a disaster. It's the hamburger. I knew that hamburger wasn't right. Samantha loves Elvis, the only thing that brings her down to the level of the other girls I have dated. When the first movie begins, she leans forward and rests her chin on the dashboard. Pure concentration. How will I survive this? I have to get out of the car—fast. I tell Samantha that I'm going for popcorn and take off at a run. When I return with the popcorn, Milk Duds, and Jujy-Fruits, Samantha hasn't moved. She reaches for the candy without looking. Her hand is apparently an antenna for sweets. I bound from the convertible again. Standing beyond the last row of cars, I wait for relief. People must be wondering about me. They probably think I'm a pervert, a Peeping Tom—everyone knows that it's out in the last rows where all the heavy action takes place. That carhop would enjoy this. I'm inventing a new dance. Maybe he poisoned me. I head back to the Continental with a Coke for Samantha. She finally turns her attention from the screen to take the drink and tells me that it's no wonder us Yankees are always complaining about the heat—Why can't we learn to be still? I love the way she says the word *still*, stretching it into two syllables. Samantha begins filling me in on the plot while I grip the edge of the seat. Fortunately, we're running low on candy. I hope Samantha's hungry tonight.

Three-fourths of the way through the last feature, I have recovered from my hamburger to the point that I can be "still." Samantha has consumed enough candy to send every dentist in Mobile, Alabama, to the mountains for the summer and enough Elvis to sit back with her head on my shoulder. She gives me a new smile, one I haven't seen before. The big fat sun I could never find in the Southern skies is in that smile. One final bad guy to be punched, a final song to be crooned, and we'll be out on the back roads with the tall pines and the Chew Mail Pouch barns, looking for the just right spot. I've practiced finding Lucky's magic button in the dark and I can do it with either hand. I hold Samantha gently. A warm, sweet wind is blowing in from the Gulf. It's sweeter than Samantha's one long dessert— sweeter than all the azalea blossoms, low-tide gumbo, mint juleps, and Coca-Cola in the whole Sweet Sunny South.